Praise for On That Day I Left My Boyhood Behind

What a remarkable story. ?" _____ ng as it was all true. I love the w _____ scene and explained the military _____ ⌐n. What an adventure Norman had, _____ ⌐d surviving the whole war unscathed. Saying tha _____ ⌐s certainly mentally scarred and probably wrote his memoirs to help exorcise some of his demons. Reading about his horse, Timbuc, almost brought a tear to my eye. Echoes of War Horse, but a real life story. A recommended book for anyone wanting to read the story of one man's, one horse's war; from the shores of Gallipoli, to the deserts of the Middle East, to the last days of the conflict on the Western Front. Well done Susan, it's a memorial to a man you must be very proud of.

Stephen Chambers. Historian of the Gallipoli Association

This is a vivid story of and by a WW1 soldier, his hopes, politics and thoughts. It is one more moving memoir of the time, helping us to understand what it felt like to be a soldier in those times. What makes this book different, however, is that Susan Burnett intersperses the personal accounts left by her grandfather with objective historical accounts. The intensely personal therefore animates the bigger history.

Yasmin Alibhai-Brown. Author, journalist and broadcaster

Published by Acorn Independent Press Ltd, 2014.

www.susanburnett.me.uk

ISBN 978-1-909121-84-3

Acorn Independent Press

ON THAT DAY I LEFT MY BOYHOOD BEHIND

NORMAN WOODCOCK
& SUSAN BURNETT

Contents

PART I: *Gallipoli*

PART II: *Greece, Egypt, Palestine and France*

About the Authors

Norman Woodcock was born in 1897 in Cudworth and grew up in Leeds where he attended the Leeds Boys Modern School. He went to war in 1914, aged 17. On his return, in 1919, he worked in local government and at the Electricity Board. He joined the National Association of Local Government Officers (NALGO) soon after starting work, and became the full time district officer for Yorkshire and the northern region in 1937. From 1939-44 he worked in the Taunton office of NALGO, then he moved back to Yorkshire.

He studied at Leeds University, gaining a diploma in public administration and becoming a Fellow of the Royal Institute of Public Administration; a Fellow of the Institute of Personnel Management; and a Fellow of the Royal Economic Society. He retired with his wife, Clara, to Buckland St Mary in 1960 and died in Netherclay House, Taunton, in 1987.

Susan Burnett was born in 1960, and grew up in Taunton where she was educated at Bishop Fox's School. She gained a degree in mathematics from Leeds University and a masters degree in health services administration from Hull University. Her career began with the Royal Institute of Public Administration Consultancy Services. Since then she has worked in the health service in England and Wales, including as a director on the board of the National Patient Safety Agency. She is now a researcher and organisational consultant working in the Patient Safety Translational Research Centre at Imperial College London. She lives in Chepstow with her husband, where they have a large vegetable garden and several bicycles.

Different fonts have been used to distinguish the two authors.

Acknowledgements

I would like to thank all those who have helped me in writing this book. Thanks go to my mother and father, Dorothy and Colin Burnett, for adding memories about my grandfather; to my sister, Ann Burnett, for reading and commenting on drafts; to my cousin, Jenny Sharrock, for her help with the photographs; to my uncle, Albert Atkinson, for explaining the horse terms; and to my friend, Janice Pavelin, for typing all my grandfather's stories. Charles Vincent and Jane Carthey provided feedback on the early drafts of the book, and their comments were a great help.

Thanks also to the staff at the Royal Signals Museum for help with the history and for the use of their photographs; to Simon Fowler for searching the National Archives; to Cherry Mosteshar for helping to edit the book; and to everyone at Acorn Independent Press for all their hard work in getting the book into print; Last but not least, thank you to my husband, Richard Lawton, for his encouragement and support.

Preface

My grandfather, Norman Marshall Woodcock, was called up on the day that war was declared in 1914. He came home five years later. For fifty years after his return he rarely spoke about what had happened but he cried each year on Remembrance Sunday. As he grew old and had time to reflect he began to write, and in time he also began to answer the questions from his grandchildren when we asked him why he was crying. Usually he told us it was about his horse, Timbuc, but it was also about what he had seen, what had happened to his friends and comrades and about the futility of the war.

I spoke to him often about what he had written, what he went through and why. In this book I have combined my memories of my grandfather's storytelling with his personal memoirs. Interspersed between his stories I have written about the history of the war in the areas where he was fighting to help set the scene.

These are my grandfather's memories and at times, although not often, they do not accord with what military historians have written since. Nevertheless, I have left the stories as he told them. He was born in 1897 and went to war as a very young man, so his views were of that time and reflected the attitude of the British Army in 1914 towards the countries that they were occupying. I have updated some of the language he used to make it more accessible today but where it helps to understand the war, I have left his language alone and hope you will read it with this in mind.

I loved my grandfather dearly and I know that he would be pleased that his story is now being shared.

Susan Burnett
June 2014

Notes to Readers

Pounds, shillings and pence

In his memoirs, my grandfather wrote about how much he earned and how much things cost in 1914. There are different ways to convert this to reflect today's value. Each method gives a different number using, for example, inflation compared to the Retail Price Index or average earnings. I have therefore left in the old money in pounds, shillings and pence. As a reference, in 1914 the prime minister earned £5,000 and a pint of milk cost the same as a pint of beer at two and a half old pennies, or tuppence ha'penny.

Yards

There are references in the book to distances in feet, yards and miles. A foot is around 30cm. A yard is 91cm, so around 10% short of a meter. A mile is 1,600 meters or 1.6km.

Place names

I have left the place names as my grandfather wrote them, for example Constantinople rather than Istanbul. I have used the old names in the history sections to match my grandfather's route through the war but, where necessary, I have also given the current names.

British forces:

In the First World War, British forces included troops from what was then the British Empire including: Australia, New Zealand, India, South Africa, the West Indies, Nigeria, Egypt and many other colonies. The term 'British forces' is used in the history books of WW1 to refer to the soldiers from all these different countries, and it is used in the same way in this book. I have made clear which countries the soldiers came from when I have been certain of the facts.

Allies

The Allies at the start of the war were: Britain, France, Russia and Serbia. Other countries joined these Allies as the war progressed, including Italy and the USA.

Central Powers:

The Central Powers were the countries in opposition to the Allies. At the start of the war these were Germany and Austria-Hungary. Other countries joined the Central Powers as the war progressed, including Turkey and Bulgaria.

Ottomans or Turks?

Like Britain and the British Empire, Turkey was at the head of the Ottoman Empire. In the book, for consistency, where I refer to Turkey and Turkish forces I am including troops from the Ottoman Empire as a whole.

The term 'tribe'

I have used the term 'tribe' with the Oxford English Dictionary definition as 'a social division in a traditional society consisting of families or communities linked by social, economic, religious, or blood ties, with a common culture and dialect, typically having a recognized leader'.

References and further reading

I have read a lot of excellent history books about the war in the region where my grandfather was; these are listed in the bibliography at the end of the book.

Photographs

I have put as many photographs as I can in the book, where I could gain approval from the copyright holder. However there are many more photographs of the events described in the book available through my web page: www.susanburnett.me.uk

Capitals

My grandfather followed the military tradition for using capitals for nouns for specific titles and army terms. I have kept his text as true to him as possible but have not used capitals in my own words, as I am a civilian and not in such practice.

Prologue

On the evening of Saturday 24th April 1915, the ships were in motion, two hundred of them. We were to land at dawn on the beach at Cape Helles on the Gallipoli Peninsula, where the village of Sedd-el-Bahr stood. The fort nearby had been shelled by the Navy and was out of action we were told. As we set off, the shore around the harbour was lined with cheering troops.

Fortunately, the sea was calm as the battleships, cruisers and destroyers towed boatloads of soldiers the 50 miles towards the beaches. I was in a boat of the battleship *Euryalis*, towed by a steam pinnace, a patrol boat. It was to be a long night.

We were surrounded by the Fleet, when at dawn, about twenty miles out, the *Queen Elizabeth* opened fire. She was the flagship and the biggest in the Fleet, carrying 15-inch guns with a range of 20 miles. We couldn't see the shells burst, but what a noise it was – rather like an express train going through a tunnel – but we could see the puffs of black, brown and white smoke they created. Then, as we came nearer, other ships joined in. Soon we saw a cloud on the horizon and the cry came 'Land Ahead'.

We saw land before the enemy opened fire. Suddenly, all hell was let loose and we were amongst it. As we moved nearer to the beach, shells were bursting overhead, in the water, on the land, everywhere, all around us. Then the fire from the Turks got heavier, until it was like hail whipping up the water. Men began shouting and crying out but in our boat all we could do was watch and wait. The troops in the forward boats jumped out into the shallower water and we saw them fall – very few made it to the beach. Then as we drew closer, our boat came under fire too.

The noise was tremendous, but I seemed to have no fear, I don't know why amongst all that noise and confusion. Then I saw my first comrade killed and the reality of what was happening came to me. A shell burst, hitting the boat and him. The boat was packed; all we could do was watch as he bled to death. His colour changed, he became whiter, the sunburn became paler. There was nothing we could do to help him. We looked at each other in the boat – some silently, some shaking, some shouting excitedly – all of us waiting our turn to land, knowing we could be next. We put his body over the side. I still see his face to this day.

A few brave souls managed to get ashore during all this, and we watched as they lay down under a low sandbank where bullets passed over their heads. Others died in the boats, crowded together. The boats drifted away full of dead and wounded.

All around our boat the sea ran red with blood.

On that day I left my boyhood behind.

PART I

GALLIPOLI

The Outbreak of War:
A Dramatic Turning Point

'Don't cry Grandpa,' I said on more than one occasion, but it was no use. His tears abated briefly as the generals appeared on the television with war medals hanging off every spare piece of khaki. It was Armistice Day 1972.

'Incompetents the lot of them,' he said. The anger in his voice aimed at the top brass was palpable. He had cried on this day every year since his return from the war in 1919. Memories of the comrades he had lost, of the horrors he had seen and memories of his horse, Timbuc.

'Why was there a war, Grandpa?'

'You need some history to understand things my dear,' he would say as he began to explain things to me. His storytelling led me to read more about the history of the war – why it started, why the British attempted a landing on Gallipoli and why the war took my grandfather to the Middle East.

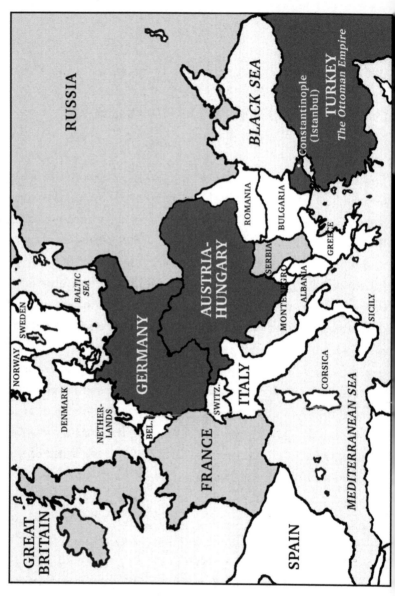

Europe in 1914 showing the countries of the Triple Entente and the Central Powers

The build up to War in 1914

At the start of the 20th century six empires ruled in Europe: Russia, Germany, Austria-Hungary, France, Britain and Turkey (the Ottoman Empire). Through treaties and agreements they were allied into two main camps referred to as the Central Powers and the Triple Entente.

The Central Powers were dominated by Germany. In 1888 Kaiser Wilhelm II came to the throne with a new vision for the country, one that expanded German influence around the world, and placed it firmly as a leading power in world affairs. This meant challenging the other leading powers on the world stage, and to do this Germany began to build up its military forces. At the same time, it began courting Turkey to gain influence in the East.

Austria-Hungary was one of the weaker powers in Europe, and was allied to Germany through a treaty drawn up in 1879 designed to protect each country should either Russia or France attack them.

The Triple Entente developed out of previous agreements and arrangements between France, Russia and Great Britain. France had been defeated by Germany in the Franco-Prussian war in 1871, and had lost territory to Germany. In the aftermath of the war, they were determined to match German military might at all costs and, after a falling out between Germany and Russia, France allied herself with Russia in an agreement that helped defend both countries in the event of an attack by Germany. Both Russia and France had agreements with Britain.

Britain's empire included a quarter of the world's population. With a strong navy, the British had undisputed control of the sea, and were determined not to lose this. So as Germany began to build its fleet, Britain did likewise. Concern over the possibility of Germany gaining control of French ports, and thus gaining access to the Atlantic trade routes, drew Britain closer to France and her defence.

Russia at the turn of the century has been described as a 'sleeping giant'. It had a population of more than 170 million, but was only slowly moving towards industrialisation. Their alliance with France brought much needed help towards this and to developing the country's infrastructure.

As Germany began to build up its military and naval might, so too did France, Britain and Russia – an arms race took place alongside the race towards industrialisation and colonial expansion.

From 1900, tension between the Central Powers and the Triple Entente grew with many crises almost tipping over into war. Germany began to consider a pre-emptive strike on France, while the Russian Army was still weak. If Germany was to be successful against France they had to act before the threat from Russia was too great – but they needed a trigger to set things off.

The Trigger

Throughout the 19th century there had been tension between the Austro-Hungarian Empire and Serbia. Within Austria-Hungary there were divisions between the German-leaning 'Greater Austria' school and the Hungarians who were more favourable to the Slavs. This led to fear amongst those in power in Vienna about the expansion of Serbia, one of the principal Slavic countries to the south of their empire. As a result, the Austro-Hungarians did everything they could to contain Serbia, while Serbia allied herself with Russia for protection.

For many years Russia had had an interest in the Balkans. As a Slavic country, Russia promoted Pan-Slavism (the unity of the Slavic people) and had developed strong links with Serbia after it gained independence from the Ottoman Empire in 1878. Russia's desire to gain control of the sea route from the Black Sea through Constantinople and the Dardanelles into the Mediterranean meant that Serbia was a useful ally in the region.

Serbia had emerged from the Balkan Wars of 1912-13 as a strong power in the region and came to be seen by the Austro-Hungarian Empire as an even greater threat. It is said that in the year following the end of the Balkan Wars, the head of the Austria-Hungary Imperial Royal Army, Conrad von Hötzendorf, proposed a pre-emptive attack on Serbia no less than 25 times, hoping to invade before Serbia had a chance to rebuild its army.

Then the trigger was pulled – literally. On 28th June 1914, Archduke Franz Ferdinand, nephew of the Emperor Franz Josef and heir to the Austro-Hungarian Empire, was assassinated by a young Serbian nationalist, Gavrilo Princip, during a visit to the Imperial Army in Bosnia. The assassination set off the chain of events that led to the outbreak of the First World War.

With German support, Austria-Hungary declared war on Serbia on 28th July 1914. This drew Serbia's ally Russia into the frame and in turn, Russia's ally France. Before either could fully mobilise their armies, Germany invaded Belgium to reach France quickly, and capture Paris 'by Christmas'. Britain made good her treaties and declared war on Germany.

Childhood Innocence:
My Life Before the War

The Portrait Specialist *Fred* 15 New Briggate ·LEEDS·

Norman in 1906, aged 9

From a very young age, I remember the rumours of the Germans invading Britain. We were told that Germany was jealous of our empire and was bent on destroying Britain. I used to read all the papers for young boys – there were many in those days, papers like the *Boys' Friend* and the *Boy's Own Paper*. They all had regular articles with titles such as, *The Great Invasion* showing pictures of German aeroplanes swooping upon us, so I was brought up to expect that we would be at war at some time soon. Indeed, in 1910 it was in the national newspapers that there was an invasion planned with a possible landing on the East Coast.

The newspapers were also full of stories of our great Naval build up. Every time Germany built a new battleship, we would build two, we were told – the big ones dreadnoughts and battle cruisers. So it was deemed patriotic to join the Territorial Army, to be trained and ready to fight. After all, you had to sign on for four years and there was no pay and the Army only lent you a uniform, so they really needed us young boys to feel patriotic and to fear Germany to get so many of us to sign on.

My brother, Joseph, joined the Leeds Rifles. I used to march alongside him when they were in town. His battalion had a band of 120 players, and it was quite thrilling when the bugles started and the whole band came in. He did four years and rose to the rank of Sergeant.

I was born in a house in Barnsley Road in Cudworth, near Barnsley, in 1897. I was the youngest of four children. Annie was the eldest, born in 1883, followed by Joseph and Winifred and me. My father was a teacher but left the profession because of poor pay. He took up a post in one of the new collieries. Later, he was appointed the first clerk to the new Cudworth Urban District Council.

Cudworth was developing at that time. Coal had been found in abundance. In fact, Grandfather Woodcock (on my father's side) and two others each put a large amount of their savings into the sinking of a pit at Carlton but they were unlucky, sinking directly on a fault where the coal was deeper on the left and high up on the right, so they halted. As they owned the land above they sold some of the coal to nearby Grimethorpe Colliery to recoup their investment. My sister kept a piece of coal about six inches across which represented grandfather's investment. In later years, Carlton Main became developed as one of the biggest collieries in England, but by that time Grandfather had gone. Imagine, if he had sunk the pit to the right we could have been very wealthy indeed.

In 1881, Grandfather Woodcock heard that the bank in Leeds, where he had all his money, had gone bankrupt and closed its doors. He went off post-haste to find out about it and, returning, had a seizure, apoplexy they said, and he fell off his horse and died.

My father drowned when I was five years old. I don't really remember much about it, but afterwards Mother said that there was no work for women in Cudworth so we had to move to Leeds. There was no widow's pension in those days. She had a cousin there whose husband had a business making and supplying surgical appliances, artificial limbs and so on. My mother was offered work helping to make surgical belts and other things. She was very good with a needle and a sewing machine. So in early 1903, we moved to Leeds, and my sister Annie obtained a teaching post at the St George's School. My mother came from a farming family. She was small in stature but had a strong, determined character. She was born in Crigglestone near Wakefield. We spent summer holidays on her brother's farm outside Leeds at Denby Grange, where my uncle taught me to ride and gave me my love of horses. My word it was fun staying on the farm. I loved playing with my cousins, and remember the times when we used to jump on and try to ride on the cows. They had hide like sandpaper and they bucked and threw you off easily.

We also used to visit my Grandfather Marshall's farm too (on my Mother's side of the family). I remember that he had boards with the names of all the cows in the milking parlour, and he used to wash and scrub his pigs every Saturday. His dog once bit my bottom.

One day I went to the field to collect the cows for afternoon milking. It was a glorious day, and out of the field the cows ambled along very slowly. I fastened the gate and followed and, rounding a corner in the quiet lane there was a sight. A picnic party had arrived and had laid out a huge white cloth all across the grass. The cows walked straight through it, one after the other, just taking a sniff at the teacups as they passed. I could do nothing but look sheepish and said nothing – I skipped past as fast as I could. They were 'townies', too frightened to shoo the cows off. My cousins called me a 'townie' because of my accent, theirs was broad Yorkshire; I used to try to talk like them when I stayed on the farm.

On the farm my uncle reared pheasants for the gentry to shoot. He taught me, at 10 years-old, how to fire a gun, and in the evenings we went out shooting rabbits. I remember my first rabbit, it was a thrill to walk up and retrieve it. There were a lot in those days; they made a good meal. I did not think then what a lot of shooting I would do in later years in the Army, or how my early training with my uncle would stand me in good stead. Certainly, I never thought that I would use a rifle to kill a man.

After saving for some time, my mother managed to buy a bakery and confectionery business in Little Woodhouse Street, in Leeds where we lived in a house over the shop. The bake house was in the basement, and we helped out. I was the boy who painted the dozens of hot cross buns with white of egg. My younger sister and I did the deliveries. My sister, Winnie, learned how to bake bread and cakes there. Perhaps I did too. When I was away in the war every time I walked past a bakery in Alexandria or Cairo or later in Jerusalem, the sight or the smell of the warm bread brought back memories of home.

So I grew up in Leeds and, in time, became a scholar at the Leeds Boys Modern School.

Leeds Boys Modern School, 1910. Norman is in the front row, second from the right

In the city horses were everywhere – working horses pulling cabs, coaches and carts. They were the taxis, buses and delivery vehicles of our day. The private cabs had an axle along the back between the two back wheels, and we used to climb underneath and sit on the bar to have a free ride. But the only way I could get to ride a horse, growing up in the city, was to make an arrangement with the stables for the Leeds Cab Company to borrow one of their horses for an hour whenever I could afford it.

The horses that pulled the hansom cabs in Leeds were muscular, and it was a thrill to climb on and ride around the streets and into the parks. They were bred to work, to be calm, so it took a real dig with the heels to get them faster than a canter. 'Don't gallop' the cabmen would shout as I left. So you can imagine that when I saw the advert calling for men to join the Territorial Army and ride every weekend, I couldn't wait. I joined as soon as I could. I was under the age to fight but that didn't seem to matter to the authorities.

I joined the Northern Signals Company of the Territorial Army, part of the Royal Engineers Signals Corps on my seventeenth birthday in January 1914. I made sure I was in a mounted unit, after all I had only joined to ride and to be with the horses.

Once I joined the TA, there was no need to borrow a horse from the cab stable. We were taught how to groom, feed and look after a horse properly. In any mounted unit the horses always come first. They were watered and fed before the men, and any man found guilty of ill-treating a horse was punished severely. The Artillery had a riding school in a building in Fenton Street in Leeds, and it was here that we went to train in the evenings and at weekends.

We learned all the skills of riding and jumping and drilling (mounted). We also learned how to drive long rein[1] two and four horses, and how to ride and drive the wagons with four and six horse teams. It was marvellous. At the time I was also taking an evening course in business at the technical school; this continued until the outbreak of war, despite both the intensive TA training and the good beer served in the Artillery canteen at *thruppence* a pint – my teetotaller's pledge was soon torn up. We had some good times in that canteen, telling tales and singing.

The training we received in Signals was comprehensive – starting with wireless. It was fascinating to find we were in direct touch with the War Office via our telescopic aerial mast, which rose to 25 feet with umbrella aerials radiating from the mast to ground. Telephones were coming in gradually but we still relied on the old technology. We used Morse code along the cables and semaphore to signal by flags. We were also trained in airline work – not flying but working up poles!

In the cable section we were trained to lay Field Cable rapidly in order to keep forces in touch with other formations. The wagons we used were, in fact, the Signal Offices with all the equipment on board to communicate along cables and lines. We had to be able to drive the wagons and horses as a team whilst running out wire from the back at a gallop.

---

[1]   'Long reining' is a term to describe how horses are trained to be driven in harness and to work in a team.

Cable wagon during training in England – photo courtesy of the Royal Signals Museum

During our weekend camps, on Sundays we practiced laying cables along the country lanes around Leeds. It must have looked a strange sight to the locals – a signals wagon with six horses, carrying drums of cable, tools, poles and signal equipment with a man riding just behind laying the cable. I enjoyed being number six in the team, the one who placed the cable in the ditch on the roadside through what was known as a 'crook-stick'. This stick was about as long as a walking stick, ash, with a metal end about three inches in diameter, not quite a circle through which the wire ran. It was exciting when going at a fast trot or canter because the wire was then running from, or to, the drum on the wagon very quickly and you had to be careful not to have it caught in the horses' legs, or your thumb. Riding like this meant that you had to hold the reins in one hand for long periods with the 'crook-stick' in the other and accommodate your speed, not to that of the wagon, but that of the wire, and if some slack came up, you had to be prepared to move off smartly to save yourself from being pulled from the saddle.

Sapper holding a 'crook stick' – photo courtesy of the Royal Signals Museum

During this time, I was also training to be an auctioneer in a firm in Leeds. My principal used to come to the office dressed in a morning coat, striped trousers, bowler hat and carrying a rolled umbrella. He came at 10am and left at 4pm, those being professional hours before the war. I could come and go to suit the work, which helped with my TA training. I worked the weekly sale and also did some rent-collecting, which really opened my eyes as a youngster to how other people lived. Many in Leeds lived in back-to-back houses with no facilities (no toilets or bathrooms) there were streets of them. Businessmen owned many of these streets, and the company I worked for managed them. We shared the rent collecting duties but I went out regularly.

Sometimes the job of rent-collecting was amusing, but often it was pathetic. I had seen poverty in the streets in Leeds but nothing like that. There were many poor, indeed desperately poor, people. I felt sorry for them, for if they could not pay the rent, after a short time, they had to leave with nowhere to go. Conditions were bad and I wanted to help but I was counselled by the company to leave well alone, which I found hard. I was sure that there was something that could be done to help these families, especially the children.

On one of my more amusing rent-collecting efforts, I knocked on the door of a small terraced house, a back-to-back I recall. A voice said, 'Come in, the rent is on the table.' The door led straight into the front room and the householder, a woman, was in a tin bath in front of the fire. I picked up the money, entered the amount in the rent book and departed, trying not to look! On another occasion, as soon as I entered the street, a woman outside the corner public house shouted, 'You'll get no b----- rent this week,' at the top of her voice. I was not sad to leave this aspect of my job when I was called up, and the poverty I had seen affected me deeply and influenced my life after the war.

Britain's War with Turkey and the Ottoman Empire

'Grandpa, why were we at war with Turkey?'

I had just bought myself a typewriter with some Christmas money and my grandfather gave me his stories to practice my typing with. Fortunately I didn't type very fast, so most of the stories in the files at home are still in his copperplate handwriting.

The Ottoman Empire and the trade routes through the Suez Canal and from Russia via Constantinople to the Mediterranean

Until the end of the 19th century being on good terms with Turkey and the Ottoman Empire had been important to Britain both for trade and for the smooth running of the Empire. Britain's trading routes to India and China were through the Mediterranean Sea and overland through Egypt (part of the Ottoman Empire) and later through the Suez Canal to ports on the Red Sea coast. Britain needed the support of the countries in the Ottoman Empire, particularly those surrounding the Mediterranean to make these trade routes safe.

There was another reason why Britain needed to be on good terms with the Ottoman Empire. Its capital Constantinople (now Istanbul) controlled the passage of goods from Russian ports on the Black Sea (via the Bosphorous) into the Mediterranean, and onwards to the trading routes used by Britain. The British did not want competition from Russian traders, so limiting Russian shipping coming through Constantinople was important, and a lot of effort was put in to diplomacy between Britain and the leaders in Turkey. Russia had long wanted to take control of Constantinople and the sea route that passed through it, and this drew Britain and France into the region and into many wars in the 19th century in support of Turkey, not least in the Crimea. Control of the sea route through Constantinople was at the root of the Gallipoli campaign.

By the 1890s – when Britain had gained control of Egypt, Cyprus and the Suez Canal and with naval bases in Gibraltar and Malta – the British Mediterranean fleet felt that the trade routes were secure. As a result, Britain lost interest in Turkey and their role as the protector and patron waned. At the same time, German interest in Turkey began to rise. This was of no particular concern to Britain at the time since it helped keep Russian interests at bay, but on this occasion the British were short-sighted.

The Germans wanted to open trade routes to the Middle and Far East to compete with British firms but were prevented by Britain from using the sea routes, so in 1903 Germany began to build an overland route – the Berlin to Baghdad railway. This led to a huge investment in Turkey, which endeared them to the Turkish authorities. As the threat of war grew, the Germans put even more effort into wooing the Turks and eventually agreed a formal alliance. This led to the Germans expanding their military mission in Constantinople. In 1913 more than 70 German officers arrived to train the Turkish Army and effectively took it over. British leaders knew this had happened and should have realised the impact this would have on the organisation of the Turkish Army, not least to their supplies of arms and ammunition.

Britain's intervention on Turkey's side in the Crimean War had given the British real popularity with the Turks despite both their expansion into Ottoman territory in Egypt and elsewhere and the large German investment in the country. British politicians therefore thought it reasonable to assume that Turkey would remain neutral in the oncoming war. Winston Churchill then did something that turned Turkish public opinion against Britain and in favour of Germany.

In 1911 Turkey ordered a dreadnought battleship to be built in England on Tyneside, called the Reshadieh. Then, when the Brazilians couldn't afford to pay for the one they had ordered, Turkey bought that one too. The costs ran to over £6million and had been funded through a nationwide campaign in Turkey with public subscriptions and special taxes, alongside Ottoman bonds issued in London. It was reported that the collection boxes in the streets of Constantinople had been filled over and over again by their patriotic citizens.

The people of Turkey were excited about the imminent arrival of their two, new modern battleships, especially since almost everyone had paid a contribution towards them. However on 2nd August 1914, before war was declared, Churchill decided to commandeer the two Turkish battleships for the British navy. This was allowed under the contract and Britain paid reparations, but the effect on the Turkish population was one of real anger. It crushed any popularity Britain had in the country, swinging popular opinion in favour of the Germans, who immediately seized the opportunity and sailed two of their warships, *Goeben* and *Breslau*, into Constantinople and handed them over to be part of the Turkish navy. The 500 Turkish sailors ready and waiting in Newcastle upon Tyne had to turn round and go home empty handed. Turkey then signed a secret agreement with Germany.

By the middle of October, with their forces being held in northern Europe, the Germans realised that this was not going to be a short war and that they needed Turkey and the Ottoman Empire with them. On the 29th October 1914, the two German warships that had arrived in Constantinople in August set sail into the Black Sea and began shelling Odessa and other Russian ports.

Russia was an ally of Britain and France, and an important one. Russian troops were fighting the Germans in northern Europe from the east, as the French and British fought from the west. With the Germans having effectively blockaded the sea route through the Bosphorous and by shelling the Russian ports, Britain's supply routes to and from Russia were closed. Scores of Russian grain ships waited in vain to get through the Bosphorous. Britain's food supply from Russia was cut off, and in exchange Britain and the Allies could no longer supply the Russians with arms. On the 2nd November Russia declared war on Turkey and the Ottoman Empire. Britain and France followed on 5th November 1914.

Britain now had new threats to consider, not just the war in France. Now there was a potential threat to the Suez Canal from the Ottoman territory to the north. Australian and New Zealand (ANZAC) forces on their way to fight in France were diverted and sent to defend the Canal.

At the same time as the politicians in Constantinople declared war on the British, the Caliph of Islam, Sultan Mehmed V, declared a jihad or holy war, urging all Muslims to join the war against the British and their allies. As will become clear later in the book, this brought trouble to the British in Egypt, particularly to the west in the Libyan Desert and to the south in Sudan. It also put fear into the leaders of the British Raj in India and led to the events in Mesopotamia, described later in the book.

Leaving for War:
What to Pack? August, 1914

Monday 3rd August 1914.

My call-up papers arrived that morning. Not long after I opened them we heard that Germany had declared war on France. I was to report to the Gibraltar Barracks in Leeds the following day. I was seventeen.

I had many things to worry about, not least what to pack. On mobilisation, the Army only supplied one khaki tunic, breeches, a cap and a pair of boots. Everything else was mine to take – so in the excitement I had to think carefully and make sure I had my underclothes, a towel, some soap, and, most importantly, some cutlery.

Tuesday 4th August 1914.

Britain declared war on Germany.

With the smell of fresh bread from our bakery in the air, I kissed my sisters, Annie and Winifred, goodbye. My mother's strength seemed to evaporate as her arms tightened around me. She found it hard to let go. It would be the last time she would hug her boy, the last time she would see him for almost five years – five years that would haunt me for the rest of my life. The man who returned would be very different from the naive, enthusiastic, smartly dressed boy who left that day in

August 1914. Throughout the war I could feel her embrace when I closed my eyes, even during the worst of times.

I reported to Gibraltar Barracks in Leeds, and met up with the lads from our TA signals unit. Me, Jones and Wilkinson became firm friends. Albert Jones was an engineering apprentice; 'Wilkie' was a pupil architect and me, 'Timber' Woodcock, a pupil auctioneer. We were all horsemen. We worked together, shared the little we had, volunteered together for any exciting jobs and groaned together when Sergeant Dick Allen got out his little book to enter our misdeeds.

Over the next two weeks we went out collecting horses from the surrounding area by day and at night we slept on the drill hall floor covered by one blanket, which was laid on a waterproof ground sheet. Grooming, feeding, watering and exercising the horses took up the remainder of our time. This was good – I was with my pals and I was working with horses.

In some Territorial Yeomanry Regiments the men actually owned their own horses and they were called up together, but this was not enough the Army needed thousands upon thousands of horses for the war effort. So we rounded up horses from the surrounding areas of Harrogate and Leeds starting with the riding schools and livery stables then moving on to businesses and private homes.

The Army had a scheme in operation before the war where they paid a yearly sum to owners who would let their animals be 'called up' and used for example in times of emergency; at annual territorial camps; or on weekend training camps. So when we called to collect their horses for the war effort there were no refusals just great sadness at having to let them go.

We heard of one family where the children had written to Lord Kitchener asking him to allow them to keep one of their horses at home, having given up two others to the war effort. Kitchener said yes but I heard of no other horses being spared; we took all that were fit to be of service.

We took everything from heavy draught animals like Clydesdales, Percherons, Shires and beautiful chestnut Suffolk Punches; to the stout and compact Galloways and Shetlands; and the fast Arabian race horses. Different breeds for different uses. The heavy draught animals were generally the most docile but the best to ride were the hunters, which were big and strong, and the Arabians which were fast. The heavy draught animals were used in six horse teams for siege guns, four and two horse teams for the lighter wagons and thousands of horses were used for the Cavalry.

After two weeks in Leeds collecting horses, we were moved to Kempston Road Barracks in Bedford. This was a collecting ground for would-be soldiers. It was like a pageant. On the parade ground were dozens of bell tents each holding twenty volunteers in Kitchener's Army – no uniforms only enthusiasm and it was rough. Lads from all walks of life were there, and it was over crowded. After two weeks, thank goodness, we were moved to Biggleswade where we occupied an old house in the town. It was very amenable with a field by the river for the horses, and the Running Stream public house for eating and for a few beers.

Northern Telegraph Units on parade in Biggleswade, 1914.
Photo courtesy of the Royal Signals Museum

One day when we were grooming there was a shout, 'A boy in the river and he's drowning'. Several of us ran across the field. There he was, floating face downwards in the middle. I dived in, and brought him to the bank, where willing hands pulled him out. We put him on his face with a pillow of a coat under his chest, and started to press the water out of him. It gushed out of his mouth. When it stopped we turned him over to raise and lower his arms to enable him to take in air. This was the Holger Nielson method of life saving we had learnt in lessons at the swimming baths in Leeds. He recovered and we carried him home, all wet of course. His mother was quite overcome and afterwards, as we went up Shortmead Street, she came out to say thank you many times. I was embarrassed at being treated like a hero when the fighting hadn't even started!

The next few weeks were spent looking after the horses, doing guard duty and practising cable laying all over Bedfordshire and parts of Hertfordshire. We also paraded in the market square and drilled. Then, later, we were billeted with the locals. We also went to Cambridge to use one of the college ranges to fire an 88 round course. I came out as a first class shot. My uncle's tuition had paid off. I wrote to my mother to tell her about my success.

Soon after being called up, a black gelding with a white star on his forehead and two white hind socks, standing proud at 16 hands, became my horse. His name was Timbuc. He was feisty and was given to me because no one else could control him. They joked that he was so feisty that he should be sent to Timbuctoo[2] – and the name stuck! Near his forequarter was a brand 'U U' with a bar underneath which showed that he had come from a ranch in America – the Wild West I was told[3]. In the American style he stayed put when the reins were dropped from his head to the ground, and he preferred a loping canter to a trot. He was a black beauty. Little did I know that this wonderful creature would be my partner in some of the most dangerous situations in the war, or that he would save my life on so many occasions.

I lived with horses for the next five years, every day, all day and often all night too. I slept beside my horse Timbuc whenever I could. I understood his moods and his wants. We understood each other. On reconnaissance his speed was vital.

---

[2]   Now spelled 'Timbuktu'.

[3]   This branding is from the UU Bar Ranch in Cimarron, New Mexico – Timbuc really was from the Wild West!

He was a lovely animal and never let me down. At the canteens in Egypt I used to buy him a string of figs – he liked them. We were together until demobilisation in 1919.

It was wet that autumn, and many of the horses we had rounded up had always been kept in stables and so had never been outside overnight. By Christmas 1914, we were losing horses rapidly due to the cold and damp so we were moved to a farm about three miles away on the Whitbread Estate in Bedfordshire, where there were open-fronted barns. Our animals had been standing out in deep mud, and for the first time they had a dry barn covered with straw to lie on – but on the first night they ate it instead!

When we were in Bedfordshire preparing for the war we practiced entraining – that is boarding everything onto a train – until we could put the whole Company outfit on board in 12 minutes. Enthusiasm was the key. During those months we ran out telephone lines all over Bedfordshire and parts of Hertfordshire for practice until we could become expert.

I think we were the premier unit in the British Army and, when the time came, we were passed out by the Director of Signals.

Our first section went to France in October 1914, but since I was too young to fight I was kept behind. Our Company expanded, and at the end of the year, as my 18th birthday approached, we began preparing for Gallipoli. Then one night we boarded the train for Avonmouth; we were off to fight. I thought of my mother and my sister Annie that night. I grew up in the care of these two remarkable women whom I always thought of as being in a class of their own. They taught me the rules of conduct, how to make friends and how to treat people. My mother said to me when I left for war, 'I have always tried to bring you up as a gentleman and I hope you always will be'. When my father died, I was really too young to remember him and I never felt deprived at any time in my life. It is really impossible to miss something you have never had, especially when you are in the care of two very remarkable women.

Norman training with the horses, Biggleswade 1914

The Origins of the Gallipoli Campaign

Countries involved in the British options to take Constantinople, showing the location of the Dardanelles

In the autumn of 1914, the idea of an offensive to take Constantinople for the Allies began to be talked about in London. This would both open the supply routes to and from Russia and would split the Turkish Army and their supply lines to Syria and Palestine, removing the threat to British interests in the Suez Canal.

This in turn would release British forces to fight in France. It was also thought that the kudos of capturing Constantinople would bring other countries into the war in support of the Allies, such as Bulgaria, which in turn would increase the supply of Allied troops and shorten the war.

Churchill and Kitchener informally discussed the possibility of a Greek Army landing on Gallipoli but the King of Greece was related by marriage to the Kaiser and did not wish to enter the war.

Rather than taking time to plan a campaign and to think through strategy and tactics, Churchill, as First Lord of the Admiralty (a political position), decided to provide a demonstration of British force to the Turks. In early November he ordered the fleet to bombard the outer forts of the Dardanelles. There were a number of direct hits. The result was said to be spectacular because the Turks had stored some ammunition above ground, and it went up with a direct hit. This gave the Mediterranean fleet false confidence that their guns could destroy the Turkish forts.

Admiral Jellicoe, the commander of the British fleet in the North Sea, called the foray up the Dardanelles and the shelling 'an unforgivable error' and other admirals called it lunacy since the main result was that it alerted the Turks and Germans to further attacks and encouraged them to improve their defences. Then, after a British submarine torpedoed a Turkish ship in the Straits, the Germans and Turks also began to increase their mine laying at the entrance to the Dardanelles.

In London, concern continued to centre on France, where the fighting had come to a deadlock. Churchill began to think about ways to use the navy to break this deadlock. There was a divergence of views in the War Council about how this could be done. Lord

Fisher, the First Sea Lord, favoured a landing on the German coast, either in the North Sea or in the Baltic. Kitchener proposed a landing at Alexandretta (now the Hatay Province, Turkey), with the objective of cutting the main line of Turkish communications. Lloyd George wanted to give support to the Serbians. But the main view in the War Cabinet was that all available forces should be focused on the Western Front in France.

There was also concern in England about sending battleships too far afield due to the threat of an invasion of British shores. German battleships had shelled the English coast around Whitby, which increased this fear. The argument between those who supported the military campaign in the west and those who supported a maritime campaign in the east was to be one of the factors that undermined the Gallipoli campaign, in particular Kitchener's desire to hold back troops and supplies for the war in France.

In the meantime, two British agents were given authority to commit the British Government to a substantial payment to bribe the Turks to pull out of the war. The negotiations failed because the British would not give a guarantee that Constantinople would remain in Turkish hands after the war.

Then on 2nd January 1915 the Russians appealed to the Allies for a demonstration against Turkey to relieve pressure on the Caucasian front. Kitchener declared that no troops would be available for a combined naval and military operation so Churchill began making plans for a naval attack alone. He sent a telegram to Admiral Carden, commander of the British Mediterranean fleet, asking whether the Dardanelles could be forced by naval gunfire alone. Carden replied that it could be done but it would be slow and he would have to have enough ships.

In 1906, the Committee of Imperial Defence considered a report prepared by the British Army general staff entitled, *The Possibility of a Joint Naval and Military Attack upon the Dardanelles*.[4] The recommendations in this report were strongly against any unaided action by the fleet alone, in fact they were emphatically against a landing on the Gallipoli peninsula altogether. When Churchill began pressing for a naval attack on the Dardanelles the secretary to the War Council, Maurice Hankey, re-circulated the papers from 1906, but the strong recommendations were ignored. It is said that the War Council were swayed by Churchill's eloquence rather than practical considerations and they gave the go-ahead.

Churchill proposed to take out the forts defending the Dardanelles gradually, sending the brand new dreadnought, the *Queen Elizabeth*, with her big guns to blast them. After the large explosion on the cliff top the previous November, Churchill was confident the naval guns would succeed in destroying the forts. Others around the table at the War Council thought differently. They knew that there was a problem of the guns firing accurately from a moving ship. There was also the flat trajectory of the guns on battleships - useful for firing at other boats at sea but no use for firing high up onto cliffs.

During January, there were arguments between the First Sea Lord, Lord Fisher, who opposed the naval operation, and Churchill, to the extent that on the 28th January the War Council met three times to discuss the issue and the history books describe the meetings as 'high drama'. Finally Churchill won the day and the naval plan was given the go ahead.

---

4   C.I.D. 20th Dec 1906 CAB 38/12/60.

On 19th February, the British fleet began their bombardment of the forts on either side of the Dardanelles. This time, as the admirals had predicted, defences were stronger and mines were everywhere. Whilst the outer forts were hit, the hidden guns inside were not. Minesweeping was slow, and, after several weeks, ammunition began to run low. Later it was found that despite one fort being hit four thousand times, none of its guns were put out of action.

The disagreements about a landing on Gallipoli to support the naval attack continued in London, but things began to change with regard to troops being available. In early February the Australian and New Zealand Army Corps (ANZAC) became available in Egypt after a failed attempt by Turkish troops, under German command, to attack the Suez Canal. Following this defeat, the Turks moved some of their troops back into the Caucasus thus reducing their threat to the Canal. Kitchener then indicated that the British 29th Division were available and the French agreed they could send a division of colonial troops from Algeria and Senegal.

Things came to a head in the War Council on 10th March with frustration about the slow progress of the navy. Kitchener announced that he had changed his mind and that troops would be sent. He immediately summonsed General Sir Ian Hamilton, Commander of the Home Forces, to his office and told him he was to command the Gallipoli campaign and Churchill wanted him to leave immediately. After quickly handing things over in London, Hamilton left the following day for Tenedos, a Greek island off the Gallipoli peninsula.

On March 11th, the Admiralty told Carden to hurry up with his naval campaign. He thought for two days and then replied that he would do what he had said he would never do – attack the Straits in daylight with his whole force. He was then taken ill.

On the 18th March, seventeen battleships headed towards the Straits, supported by cruisers, destroyers and minesweepers. In the battle that followed the British and French lost 700 men and six battleships – three sunk and three crippled. Very few of the Turkish guns were put out of action. It did not take long for the realisation that the navy were not going to be able to force the Straits. Constantinople was out of their reach. If there was to be progress then a land force was needed.

The invasion of Gallipoli was on.

Off to Egypt, A Land I'd Only Read About, 1915

It was a sight on the dock at Avonmouth – it was evening and there were dimmed lights everywhere. It was busy with people, horses and carts and supplies that were being loaded onto the ships. In the darkness we could just make out the rigs and jigs that were in motion, and we could hear them squeaking and creaking as they swung, loaded, from shore to ship and back, empty. Ships gangways were full of men pushing loaded carts on board, shouting to each other as they bounced over the boards.

We rode in the dark up to the side of a big ship at the quay and dismounted, put our saddles and blankets in sacks and waited in turn to take our horses up the gangway. I had never taken a horse on a ship before. Although we had, many times, practiced boarding trains with horses and wagons in a minimum time, I was quite nervous. Ahead of me some horses were difficult whilst others were docile and easy to lead.

The lights surrounding the ship were low but just enough to see the way up the ship's gangway, not the whole ship – an unreal feeling. As we began the walk towards the entrance I wondered if Timbuc would shy and refuse to go up but I needn't have worried for he followed me, clattering on the boards and nudged me in the back as if to say 'hurry up'. It was up and round and down into the bowels of the ship clattering on iron plates. Below it was dark and claustrophobic. Each horse had little room, only 2ft 3inches (70cm) in width between each bar. They couldn't lie down during a voyage, cruelty really, they stood with their heads out of the stall and watered and fed in a metal trough in front of each one.

Not long after boarding our ship, numbered 1,022, left the quay and stood out into the Bristol Channel to wait for the convoy. Next day we sailed. I was seasick almost immediately, and this lasted until just before we arrived at Gibraltar. Destroyers had escorted us there but there was no trouble with German ships.

During the voyage, we groomed the horses as far as possible and lavished affection on them at all times. Often, if one of us was missing from a parade on deck, we would be found with the horses below, tending them. At first, when we were cleaning out, we pushed the manure out of the boat but this was stopped because it left a long trail in the sea which the enemy submarines saw and followed. So we left it where it was and got used to the smell. At the end of a voyage, the horses stood in a foot or more of manure, but surprisingly seemed not to suffer from it in any way.

After Gibraltar on our way to Malta, the ship pitched instead of rolling as it had been doing before and I was sick again. I was miserable. The food wasn't the best, and anyway I couldn't keep it down. My pals laughed and teased me but couldn't cheer me up.

At Malta we took on coal. It was all very primitive, surprisingly so I thought, given our industrial might and our Navy. Men appeared with a small basket of coal each, walked up the gangway, emptied the coal down a hole in the deck then walked back in a continuous stream all night and next morning.

The next morning the sea was beautifully green, and floating just below the surface of the water were big lumps of coal dropped by our loaders. Some of it had probably been dropped on purpose, for as we watched a fleet of small boats came from the shore with men rowing and small boys swimming to retrieve the coal. The locals were clearly quite delighted.

After calling at Malta, we set off for Alexandria where we would arrive a fortnight later. The journey through the Mediterranean was wonderful, with beautiful weather and calm seas. What made it truly wonderful were the dolphins. They appeared all around our boat and came with us, often seeming to play in the bow wave. We couldn't believe our eyes at first, having only seen pictures of these wonderful creatures in books at school.

On the way to Alexandria I was asked by my comrades if I would swim against a young man who said he was breast stroke champion of Yorkshire and they, not believing him, had said they would find someone to beat him. He did not belong to our unit so I did not know him but I agreed and the first port we went to was to be the one for the competition – that happened to be Alexandria. I had learned to swim in the baths in Leeds, where I had become a strong swimmer. All was arranged, the Captain of the ship was to be the starter and we had to swim from one quay to another. It all looked easy as we dived in. But I had never experienced anything like it.

The water was full of rubbish – boxes, manure and bottles. I ploughed through to the quay, got out and was sick – it was horrible. When I finally looked back the other chap had given up half way. Never again did I swim in a dock. My pals were delighted, they had won money with my victory and promised to buy me a beer when they next could. I needed more than a beer!

We disembarked in Alexandria and took the horses ashore. When we arrived with the horses at a port there were not always facilities for loading and unloading other than 'slinging' on or off. The sling was the width of the horses' belly. It was strange to stand in the bowels of a ship looking at the square patch of light above the open hatch, when suddenly a horse in a sling appeared and then down he came to finally stamp his feet on the iron deck (or sometimes onto our toes); or waiting on a barge as the horse appeared fastened to the yard arm of the ship's crane and gradually turning as he came towards us. We became experts at this loading and unloading, ship to ship, ship to barge or ship to shore.

Horse being 'slung' off a ship
Photo source: Central Press, Hulton Archive, Getty Images ©

Our horses had been cooped up for two weeks, standing in one position, not even being able to lie down. So when they were put on the quay their knees sagged. It was very sad to see them so weak, especially my Timbuc. It took a lot of love and care to get the horses back to their full strength.

In Egypt we were taken up to Chatby-les-Bains, the French suburb of Alexandria, for a few weeks where mainly French people lived. Along the coast at Alexandria there were suburbs where the different nationalities lived – first the Maltese then Italian, French, Greek, English and, finally, at Sidi Bishr, the furthest point, was one of the Sultan's palaces, and wonder of wonders, there was a tramway on raised rails running from Alexandria along the coast, with stops every half mile.

The electric motors and tramcars were all made by Dick Kerr of Preston, Lancashire. There were 1st, 2nd and 3rd class cars with special ladies' compartments that had ground glass screens. Two or three trams travelled coupled together, the conductors blew horns to start or stop as a signal to the driver who sat in a cabin. In Leeds, before I left for the war, our drivers stood in front of the tram in the rain or snow in vehicles made by the same firm. What misers we were in England with little regard for the working-man's welfare.

Alexandria was indeed an interesting town: modern shops, wide streets and a general air of prosperity. Although we saw many other towns afterwards, few were better than Alexandria. There was a considerable French presence, as in Egypt generally, although the town was quite cosmopolitan. It had a very mixed population, and we were told there was rivalry between the different groups.

It was all quite different from Leeds. I remember going to the opening of the first picture house in Leeds, the Theatre de Luxe in Kirkgate. For two pennies we had a seat and a cup of tea in the interval. Just off Kirkgate was an arcade where a chap called Spencer had a penny bazaar where, very occasionally, if we had any money we might buy something, a clay pipe for example. There was a Jewish boy in the open market nearby and they joined up as Marks and Spencer. We children were their first customers.

We sampled the local Egyptian food, and not knowing the money meant that we were taken in by the locals and they made a bob or two from us, but we had little money to buy anything. My pay was ten shillings and six pence a week, out of which I allotted three shillings and sixpence to my mother. The government made that up to four shillings and eight pence and continued it at that rate until I was demobbed at 22 years of age.

After several enjoyable weeks in Chatby-les-Bains, it was announced that we were to return to Alexandria. We were to embark on a ship for Mudros, on the Greek island of Lemnos in the Aegean Sea, to prepare for the landings on Gallipoli at Cape Helles. I remember the feeling of excitement when we were told. We had heard the rumours about the landings and had been given some information, so when we were told that we were to set sail the anticipation was immense.

General Hamilton's Preparations for the Gallipoli Landings

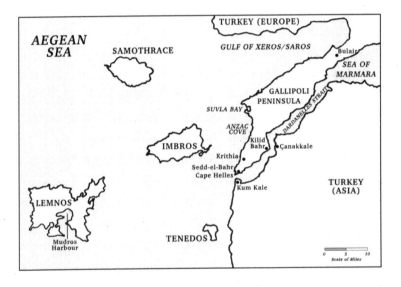

The Gallipoli Peninsula, the Dardanelles and the surrounding islands used by the British

After being told he was to command the military force to support the fleet in the Dardanelles, General Ian Hamilton wrote in his diary: 'My knowledge of the Dardanelles was nil; of the Turk nil; of the strength of our own forces next to nil'. Kitchener expected him to leave the room after being told of his new command, but

Hamilton began asking questions. Kitchener's answers were: 'no' to more troops; 'no' to submarines to stop the Turks re-supplying their forts by sea; 'no' to army aircraft; and 'no' to landing on the Asian side of the Straits. When asked about the enemy's strength, Kitchener replied: 'Be prepared for 40,000'. How many guns? No one knew. In addition, there would not be the usual 10 per cent extra margin of reserves to fill casualties.

Hamilton left for Dover the next day with: an out of date map, two short guidebooks, a textbook from 1912 about the Turkish Army and a pre-war report on the Dardanelles defences. He had no staff apart from his chief of staff, Major General Braithwaite. In his diary, Hamilton made clear his frustrations at the lack of plans for an amphibious attack, writing: 'The Dardanelles and the Bosphorous might be in the moon for all the military information I have got to go upon' and 'There is no use trying to make plans unless there is some sort of material, political, naval, military or geographical to work upon'.

Despite all the talk of a landing on Gallipoli no one in London had made any plans, nor had they drawn together any intelligence on the terrain or the strength of the opposition's forces. Hamilton was further frustrated by not having suitable staff to assist him, saying:

My Staff still bear the bewildered look of men who have hurriedly been snatched from desks to do some extraordinary turn on some unheard of theatre. One or two of them put on uniform for the first time in their lives an hour ago. Leggings awry, spurs upside down, belts over shoulder straps! I haven't a notion of who they all are.

It is almost unbelievable. At least you would have expected a strong team to be put together to work on the plans for such a crucial invasion. Military historians have commented since that Hamilton's briefing was completely inadequate and was in effect a gross dereliction of duty on the part of the army general staff. General Hamilton arrived on the Greek island of Tenedos at 3pm on 17th March 1915, just after Admiral Carden had left after being taken sick with what are now thought to have been stress-related stomach ulcers. Hamilton observed the failed attack by the fleet the next day. This made the landings certain. He toured the Gallipoli peninsula on a boat and viewed the shore through his binoculars, then he set off to look at the Greek island ports to be used in the landings.

During the early stages of the naval campaign, Rear-Admiral Wemyss had visited the island of Lemnos to look at the facilities for naval ships and troops in the harbour of Mudros. He reported that there was very little water on the island, and that whilst Mudros was a wonderful natural harbour there were no berths where ships could load and unload. This meant that all the loading and unloading had to be done by small rowing boats. He realised that for a landing on Gallipoli they would need a large base there since Egypt was too far away. There needed to be hospitals, ammunition depots, rest camps, a safe water supply and a road system. The resources to create all this were non-existent. The seeds of the nightmare ahead were growing.

Hamilton arrived in Alexandria on the 26th March 1915. He had three weeks to get everything ready for the largest amphibious landing on hostile shores ever undertaken. His full complement of administrative staff still hadn't arrived to help with the plans. They eventually arrived on the 11th April.

The next few days and weeks were a mad rush to get all the items needed for the planned invasion, which required a lot of improvisation. Men were sent to the shops and bazaars of Alexandria and Cairo to buy all sorts of things that had not been shipped from England. For example, since they were not sure about whether there was a source of water on Gallipoli they needed to buy lots of receptacles that could hold water. They also needed extra boats, especially small boats to work between ships and between the ship and the shore. Donkeys were needed to move provisions once they landed. Periscopes were needed in the event of trench fighting. Maps were bought from shops that sold guidebooks about Turkey.

The ships that arrived from England had not been packed for a landing, so everything had to be taken off and re-packed in the right order. This took up valuable time and went on under gas lights all night, every night. It soon became evident that there was a shortage of the essentials such as guns and ammunition but all requests from Hamilton to Kitchener received a short 'no'. As a result, the army set up workshops to make hand grenades and trench mortars.

Hamilton realised that there was also a shortage of troops. It is said that he did not ask Kitchener for more men because he had promised not to embarrass him with such requests. Several divisional commanders preparing for the invasion, not least Hunter-Weston, who commanded the 29th Division, thought that the obstacles were too great for the landings to go ahead, but there was no choice, the orders had been given.

On top of the supplies problems, Hamilton also faced the fact that the landings would be of absolutely no surprise to the Turkish and German forces. The press in Egypt reported all the activities of the British in their newspapers and traders took information from the Egyptian ports back to Greece to be passed on to the Turks. Letters from England arrived in the post addressed to the 'Constantinople Force'. Nothing was secret. Hamilton hoped that the Turks might think that this was a cover and that perhaps the real landings would be elsewhere, but it was only a hope. The Turks with the Germans had had plenty of time to prepare for the landings; they had built roads, strengthened gun fortifications and dug trenches. Most importantly they had had time to organise and train the Turkish troops.

From mid-April troops from Britain, Australia, New Zealand and France together with colonial forces from Senegal and Algeria were taken by boat to Mudros in readiness for the landings. The first wave of troops were due to leave Mudros on 20th April but the weather prevented them leaving.

Troops already in ships anchored outside Mudros harbour suffered badly from seasickness, while they waited for calmer seas. In the meantime, seaplanes bombed an area on the European side of the narrows. This had the very unfortunate effect of driving up to 2,000 Turkish troops towards the beach where the Australian and New Zealand forces were to land.

From Alexandria to Mudros: Preparing for the Landings

Once we were told were leaving we couldn't stop talking about the landings, about what it would be like and what we might experience. None of us had ever left England before but we had all read adventure stories and seen pictures of the Orient in books at school. We conjured up some vivid images of what it would be like to land on a foreign shore and fight the Turks on the way to Constantinople.

Our journey from Alexandria over the Aegean Sea to the island of Lemnos was uneventful. Thankfully it was a calm sea and I wasn't seasick. Not many submarines had been seen there at that time, but everyone was still fearful and we kept a good watch for them.

Eventually, we arrived in Mudros harbour, and what a sight met our eyes. The harbour was very large, like a huge lake, and it was full of ships, battleships, cruisers, destroyers and smaller craft passing between and round them. It was a hive of noise and activity. There were huge hospital ships from the White Star line, Cunard, and Union Castle, all painted white with green lines round them and huge red crosses on their sides. We could see hundreds of troopships full of soldiers many on deck who waved as we passed. There were tugs, big barges, small ships, all with smoke pouring from their funnels. . All around them there were small boats travelling from ship to ship and ship to shore.

On shore we could see men marching and drilling, and there were wagons and horses everywhere with piles of stores stacked up on any available piece of land. There was activity everywhere and to cap it all bands were playing in several locations which made for quite a lively atmosphere. We landed and joined the throng.

As a self-contained unit capable of undertaking any type of signal work we formed part of General Headquarters Signal Company and were attached to the 29th Division.

There were about 75,000 troops from England; 30,000 from Australia and New Zealand; a French Division of 16,000; also a Naval Division[5] of about 16,000 and around 16,000 horses and 300 vehicles. All these were to be landed on a hostile shore to beat the Turks at, what we later found, was their strongest point and after they had been given notice of our intentions to land by our preparatory activity in Egypt. This had given them plenty of time to prepare for our arrival with barbed wire and guns. The whole exercise was planned in three weeks by an untrained staff. But we didn't know any of this then.

It would have been good to have been able to take some pictures of the harbour in Mudros when we arrived it was so spectacular, but we were not allowed to have cameras, a foolish ruling by our Supreme Command. It was a crime to have one and we were threatened with a Court Martial if we disobeyed this order. That is why so few photographs were taken. Fortunately, the Australians refused to obey this English order and that is

---

[5]   Now the Royal Marines.

why many of the photographs appeared subsequently. We English soldiers admired the Australians attitude to their British Officers, they were not backward in speaking up about stupid rules and had a camaraderie such that they knew that if one disobeyed a rule with good justification then the other men would support them.

What the British Generals failed to realise was that we were not regular soldiers who had been paid the King's shilling to sign on. Many of the volunteers and the TA soldiers had brains as good as (and often better than) the Generals. Many of my comrades, in civilian life, were scientists, teachers, and radio and wireless experts – the sort of people the regular Army had never had cause to meet in their previous Army days. We soon realised that before the war, the military hierarchy had a lot of leave, little work and plenty of spare time, which they spent taking tea with the ladies – not learning about new methods of warfare.

The Officers tried to impress themselves upon us with orders and regulations, having little else to impress us with. Indeed, in the Signals our Territorial Officers were infinitely better at the communications work than any Army regular. One reason was that regular Army Signal units had not developed beyond the flags and lamp stage. A soldier did 2 years with the colours and 10 or more on reserve. Our Territorial unit was composed mainly of post office workers, men who knew about radio and wireless and were experts in telegraph work. At home our key operators routinely did messages at thirty words a minute. The Army rate was twelve, the Navy fourteen!

The day after our arrival on Mudros there was a call for volunteers – 'Anyone who could row a boat'. Along with others, I volunteered – it sounded like a bit of fun. We went down to the landing stage where there was a boat. It was a huge rowing boat with six oars, long ones, on each side. We had to row out to a depot ship in the middle of the harbour, called the *Tintoretto*, to collect bales of blankets and bring them back to the shore. Apparently this was the only way of transferring things from ship to shore since there was nowhere for ships to dock. It took us a long time dodging round anchor chains, getting out of the way of ships' propellers as they came and went. There was a lot of moaning and groaning in our boat. We loaded our boat and rowed back, vowing that we wouldn't say anything when we got back, we would leave it for the next lot to find out what a horrible job it was; we weren't going to do it again.

The next day there was a call for volunteers 'who could row', but word had got around from other boats and no one answered the call so the order changed to: 'Fall in those men who rowed the boat yesterday'. So we went again, but it took all morning. We won the slow rowing race, complaining that our arms ached.

General Hamilton's Plans for the Gallipoli Landings

General Hamilton's plans were simple: to land at dawn with the main British force on three beaches at the base of the peninsula, V, W and X beaches. French troops were to land on the Asiatic side at Kum Kale for a short period to divert attention and to put the Turkish guns out of use so that they could not fire on the landing beaches on the opposite shore. Y and S beaches were added as extra landing beaches to provide a covering force from each side, intended to be part of a pincer movement in support of the landings on V, W and X beaches. A separate strong ANZAC force was to land at Z beach, 12 miles to the north of Y beach and on the same side, pushing on across the Peninsula and cutting off Turkish troops in the south.

The troops were to be loaded into cutters and other vessels, towed as far onto the beaches as possible and then rowed to the shore for the final approach. In addition, on V beach, 2,000 troops were crammed in to the *SS River Clyde*, a collier that had been converted to enable troops to run down steps on each side once the boat had been grounded ashore. It was an idea based on the wooden horse of Troy.

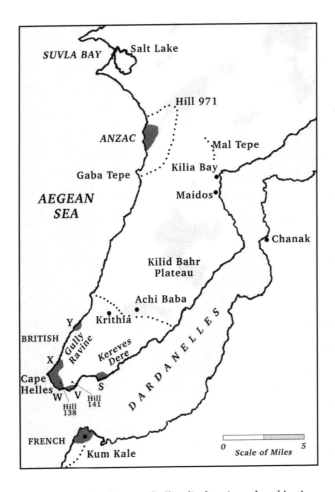

The landing beaches on Gallipoli showing the objectives and area actually taken

Back in England, Maurice Hankey, Secretary of the War Council, began to have severe concerns about the landings. In the middle of March he sent a letter marked 'secret' to the prime minister, Herbert

Asquith, in which he set out his concerns and listed the questions that needed to be answered to assure the War Council that the landings would be successful. The letter started with a reminder about how previous combined military and naval attacks had failed when there had been inadequate planning. He also reminded the prime minister that the great advantage of surprise had been lost, and that the Turks and Germans had been reinforcing the Peninsula for some time, making the military enterprise 'formidable'. His list of questions included: the number of troops needed, the plans for landing piers to get supplies ashore, the arrangements for water and whether the naval guns were adequate as heavy artillery.

The letter finished as follows: 'Unless details such as these, and there are probably others, are fully thought out before the landing takes place, it is conceivable that a serious disaster may occur'

The War Council considered Hankey's memorandum but no action was taken. The rest, as they say, is history.

The Day I Left My Boyhood Behind, 25ᵗʰ April, 1915

Naval steam pinnace towing boatloads of soldiers – Mudros Harbour 1915

Immense enthusiasm pulsated throughout the forces in the harbour at Mudros. We were all excited about the adventures ahead and, with the sight of so many ships around us, it seemed certain to be a success. The troops scrawled slogans on the ships' sides, 'Turkish Delight' and 'To Constantinople and the Harems'. They lined the decks cheering and shouting to arrivals and departures. It had quite a holiday spirit, which we all got caught up in it. Kitchener had said that the sight of one British Sergeant with a Union Jack would frighten all the Turks. We believed him but soon found out that he was wrong.

Then came the time for the landings.

We climbed into the boats that would take us across the Aegean to Gallipoli. Earlier, we had been given our extra rations including water and ammunition, and we had loaded our signals equipment. Our boat was from the battleship *Euryalis* and we were towed by a steam pinnace (a patrol boat). On the evening of Saturday 24th April 1915, the ships were in motion, two hundred of them. We were to land at dawn on the beach at Cape Helles on the Gallipoli Peninsula, where the village of Sedd-el-Bahr stood. The fort nearby had been shelled by the Navy and was out of action, we were told.

As we set off, the shore around the harbour was lined with cheering troops. We waved and cheered too. There was a sense of adventure in the air.

Fortunately, the sea was calm as the battleships, cruisers and destroyers towed boatloads of soldiers the 50 miles towards the beaches. It was to be a long night.

We were surrounded by the Fleet when, at dawn, about twenty miles out, the *Queen Elizabeth* opened fire. She was the flagship and the biggest in the Fleet, carrying 15-inch guns with a range of 20 miles. We couldn't see the shells burst but what a noise it was – rather like an express train going through a tunnel – although we could see the puffs of black, brown and white smoke they created. Then, as we came nearer, other ships joined in. Soon we saw a cloud on the horizon and the cry came: 'Land Ahead'.

We saw land before the enemy opened fire. Then suddenly all hell was let loose, and we were amongst it. As we moved nearer to the beach, shells were bursting overhead, in the water, on the land, everywhere, all around us. Then the fire from the Turks got heavier until it was like hail whipping up the water. Men began shouting and crying out but in our boat all we could do was watch and wait.

The troops in the forward boats jumped out into the shallower water and we saw them fall – dragged down by their kit, very few made it to the beach. Then as we drew closer, we were set free by the pinnace and our boat came under fire too.

The noise was tremendous but I seemed to have no fear; I don't know why amongst all that noise and confusion. Then I saw my first comrade killed and the reality of what was happening came to me. A shell burst, hitting the boat and him. The boat was packed and all we could do was watch as he bled to death. His colour changed – he became whiter as his sunburn became paler. There was nothing we could do to help him. We looked at each other in the boat – some silently, some shaking, some shouting excitedly – all of us waiting our turn to land, knowing we could be next. We put his body over the side. I still see his face to this day.

There was a fort just above the sea, on the right, and we watched as the walls were hit by shells from our battleships. Frustratingly, we had nothing to fire at from our boat because we couldn't see a target within range. The beach looked about 300 yards long, covered with rows and rows of barbed wire along its entire length. At the top of the beach we could see that there was a line of trenches with earth on top and firing bays in front in which were machine guns and pom-poms (guns firing large explosive shells). It was said later that there were 700 guns of various calibres trained on that beach where we were to land, V beach on Gallipoli.

A few brave souls managed to get ashore during all this, and we watched as they lay down under a low sandbank where bullets passed over their heads. Others died in the boats, crowded together and the boats drifted away full of the dead and wounded.

Many strange things happened because men persisted in doing what they had been told to do. A sailor managed to pole his cutter up to the beach, but when he turned to beckon his passengers to the shore he saw they were all dead and wounded. Then we watched as he was hit and his boat slipped back into the sea and was sunk. Some in the sea were alive because they clung to their boats as they went overboard and they hung on in the water hoping to get ashore. All was confusion but still I did not feel afraid. I felt quite calm, I don't know why, strange really – I can only describe it as like being in a wonderland.

A ship named the *River Clyde* was packed with a brigade of the 29th. The plan was for her to be grounded onshore and for the troops to run ashore from the holes cut in her sides and down the stairways mounted along her sides. Amongst all the shot and shell, she did not quite make it to shore. We watched from our boat as many ran down the stairways into deep water and were drowned. Amidst the awful turmoil, sailors dragged barges around her front to form a sort of quay for landing. Men were falling everywhere. Bodies were floating everywhere.

Around our boat the sea was red with blood. It was an awful, awful sight.

As we approached the shore, the current running down the Dardanelles and into the Aegean, which was strong at about 20 knots, caught our boat. We had been cut off from the boat that was towing us. There was nothing we could do but gradually drift to the left, away from where we were supposed to land.

We had been issued with an extra 100 rounds of ammunition and three days' rations of food and water (one full water bottle). All our kit was heavy, too much for deep water, and the idea of jumping into the sea didn't appeal – we knew we would sink immediately with all our gear on. Plenty of men had jumped in, and their bodies were floating all around our boat.

Slowly, we drifted until we were under a cliff where it was like a Sunday afternoon with only the sound of battle on our right. We were stranded, so we sat there and waited to be collected. All day we waited in the heat, watching as the battle went on. There were discussions as to whether we should try to swim to the shore but we had heavy equipment and would surely sink. Then, as it got dusk, a boat hailed us and we were towed back to a collecting point for the next day's attack. We were told that only about a dozen men were alive on our beach by then. No one spoke of it in our boat but we all knew we had been saved by the current.

Meanwhile, on the other beaches, progress had been made. They were ashore at Morto Bay, X beach and W beach. However, there were also tremendous casualties.

Next day, on our beach, it started again. A soldier stepped from the sheltering sandbank and started, with utter coolness, to cut a road through the barbed wire amidst an absolute hail of fire. We could see his clothes being shot off him in tatters but he carried on. When our boys tried to go forward again, they ran through the gap that he had made. He was wounded in 42 places and awarded a V.C[6]. Poor, brave chap died in hospital later in Cairo.

Gradually, the Turks' fire died down and we got ashore. Gunfire was still heavy but rifle fire was down to an occasional burst. As we worked up to the top of the beach, we reached the trench at the top, which had a cover over it, and we found our boys pulling rifles from the hands of the Turks inside. Then someone shouted: 'Round the back!'. Over the top and round the sides we all went. To my recollection, none of the Turks came out alive.

As we fought, men stopped to help others, trying to staunch the flow of blood from the limbs of their comrades who had been shot or blown to pieces – men with parts of their legs missing who were hopping or crawling to find shelter. Bodies everywhere.

Meanwhile, help came from W beach, on our left, and eventually resistance was overcome. Very heavy shells still came from the Asiatic shore to our right but, although a few men were killed, they did little damage because we heard them coming and fell flat when they burst. We quickly learned to take cover, although there wasn't much. The trees onshore were small and there weren't many. In places, the ground had been cultivated.

---

[6]   The Victoria Cross (V.C.) is the highest award available to the armed forces for gallantry. It is awarded for an act of outstanding courage or devotion to duty in the presence of the enemy.

We had not run out any telephone lines so far. Indeed, we did not know where our stuff was so there was no communication with the Generals in charge, no orders as to what to do next. Then the Turks began to retreat and we followed up as far as the village of Krithia, a small village under Achi Baba hill, which dominated the country where we were held. We were exhausted. We had little ammunition left and no water. We had eaten nothing. We waited. Fighting grew heavier and, exhausted, we stopped.

We were short of ammunition as none had come ashore and we hadn't any transport. No one knew what we should do, there was confusion. Then the cry came: 'Dig in!', 'Enver Pasha coming down from Constantinople with 30,000 hand picked men', 'Orders to drive you into the sea'. Englishmen didn't like digging and the ground was hard. We thought that to dig a trench a foot deep was sufficient protection and we were tired, hungry and thirsty. What is more we didn't have the equipment to dig in this terrain.

Mercifully, firing died away and we could sit and take stock. We had time to eat the meagre rations we had been given. Our iron rations were handy though the biscuits, like dog biscuits at home, were dry and hard to swallow with no water and one tin of bully beef to five men was just a snack[7].

---

[7] On landing, each soldier was issued with 'iron rations', a term used to describe the food issued to troops for emergency purposes when they would be cut off from the usual supply channels. In 1914 it comprised preserved meat, cheese, biscuits, tea, sugar, salt and meat extract (often in the form of an OXO cube). During the landings, seawater got into many soldiers iron rations and rendered much of it inedible.

The NCOs[8] must have had an idea of what was to come, they were harder and passed along the line shouting, 'Dig in, your lives depend on it!'. But we were weary and one foot seemed deep to us.

We didn't know what was coming.

That night, at about ten o'clock, the attack started, first on our right, then spreading across the front lasting until daylight. It began with a stuttering of rifle fire and occasional machine gun fire with some guns at first from their side. Then our Navy joined in, firing at first well beyond us but then some shells began to fall amongst us and we had no way of communicating back to ship to tell them.

We soon realised that the Navy were useless in supporting an attack on land because the British Navy did not possess a Howitzer of any size. In consequence, all their shells burst in the air or on impact with the ground. The trench beat them. They had to actually see their targets to fire effectively and then, on occasions, they could not hit them. I watched as a ship tried firing at a lighthouse used by the enemy as a look out. It took 22 rounds to hit it and another 20 to destroy it, and it stood out on top of the cliff in full view. Communications from ship to shore were primitive, by semaphore flags during the day and lamps at night, so often they fired into the troops, not knowing exactly where they were.

Then the real attack came, German fashion, men shoulder to shoulder firing from the hip. Fortunately, a lot of it passed over our heads, not being aimed. Our rifles and fire were better but

---

[8]   A non-commissioned officer (NCO) is someone who has risen through the ranks of the army, to the position of officer, rather than receiving a commission.

our line was thin and we were short of ammunition. We took ammunition from any man killed. It is impossible to describe some of the happenings because some men were afraid and others excited, some were quite mad. There was dreadful execution of our enemy on the first two attacks, but we were sadly outnumbered. Gradually, it became a mix up and small groups of us continued – with bayonets coming into use. On one occasion the Turks and Germans came into the attack and, as we had no cover, we stood up to fire. One Turk ran forward, jumped and bayoneted one of our boys but as the Turk had jumped he had landed on our boy's feet and so he could not fall over until they both fell together. As they did so, another of ours bayoneted the Turk, and they died as though in one another's' arms.

Before long, our retreat began towards the beaches. We went back to almost the beach heads. Both sides were tired. Firing died away and the enemy retreated too. We could not do anything more. Every unit was mixed up. We ended up with the Munster Fusiliers and a big, raw-boned Irish Sergeant was swearing as he urged us to stand.

Many times afterwards I thought of what I had seen and heard but could not speak of to anyone. They wouldn't believe it. As we fought, the ground around us had filled up with bodies; those who fell as they died, some killed by gunfire but most through hand to hand combat. The noise of dying is something else that has stayed with me.

That night, on a five mile front, we lost 10,000 men who were killed and wounded. The enemy losses were greater than ours and their attack was over. Both sides dug in.

We finished up half a mile from the beach. This was our nearest shave to being pushed into the sea where we would all have perished. The execution we did with our rifles was our saviour but we finished, without ammunition, in hand to hand combat. No ammunition had come ashore. In the next eight months fighting, we did not get back into Krithia and we had an attack every fortnight and a bigger attack every month. At the end there were nine of us left in our section.

The Peninsula was about five miles wide rising to a hill called Achi Baba, which was around five miles inland. From the sea this hill, shaped like a head and shoulders across the land, dominated all the landings. It was obvious once we were ashore that this was about the worst place anyone could have picked for an amphibious adventure as it was bare, with no shelter anywhere. It was within sight of a hostile shore in Asia, and within range of heavy guns at Chanak just up the narrows of the Dardanelles. What is more, the nearest British base was Mudros – 50 miles away by sea and many miles from bases in Egypt from where everything had to be shipped through a sea patrolled by German submarines. There was no port anywhere near from where stores, guns, ammunition etc. could be landed and, most importantly for us soldiers, there was no fresh water.

So we were ashore in the most awful of conditions and had to make the best of it. In two days I went from a young recruit with a mind full of wonder and imagination about the glory of battle from the books I had read as a youngster, to a battle-hardened soldier who had fought and killed with rifle shot and bayonet. In two days I felt that I had seen all the horrors of war – but there was more to come.

The Landings: An Historical Account

That day, the French landed at Kum Kale on the Asiatic side and put the Turkish guns out of action as planned. Having achieved their objectives, they withdrew.

The ANZAC forces were swept by the current, which took them 1.5 miles (2.5km) further north of Z beach, where they had planned to land. They landed instead on a beach surrounded by steep cliffs rising to a height of 200 feet (60 metres). By 5:30am, 4,000 men had landed. The Turkish troops defending the area were few – a single company – and they were over-run quite quickly. The plan was then for the ANZACs to cross three small ridges, to capture the main hill – Hill 971 – and to take control of the valley that cuts across the Peninsula leading to the town of Maidos on other side of the Peninsula near the Straits.

Taking this hill and valley would cut off the Turkish supply lines to the south. The officers had meticulous orders to this effect but not knowing that they had landed in the wrong place, they proceeded into the countryside behind the cliffs where they found a jumble of valleys and ridges running in different directions. Inevitably, with poor maps, they were confused by the terrain.

General Birdwood, who was in charge of the ANZAC landings, made camp on the beach and tried to direct the battle from there with very poor communications to the frontline. Mustafa Kemal, who was leading the Turkish forces, realised the importance of preventing the Allied forces advancing across the Peninsula, and personally led the regiment of troops he had in the area into an attack on the ANZAC forces, ordering his troops to die for their country. The attack was successful. The ANZAC forces were stopped and were confined to a semicircular area stretching about a mile or so inland from the beach.

In his command centre on the beach, General Birdwood received information from those coming back from the front and, rather than going to see for himself, he was swayed by the reports that they were outnumbered by Turkish troops and would be pushed into the sea if there was a mass advance. They dug in. History now shows that throughout that day there were double the numbers of ANZAC to Turkish troops in the area.

On Y beach the defences were few and far between. The Turks had considered this a most unsuitable area for a landing. British forces landed at dawn with no opposition. Having landed, they did nothing for twelve hours. The colonel in charge walked to within 500 yards of Krithia, which was unoccupied at the time, walked back to his lines and rested. The excuse for inaction was said to be the orders, which told him to capture the guns (there weren't any) and then to join the British forces advancing from X, W and V beaches. The Colonel in charge did send a message to X beach to ask if he should come down or wait to meet them but receiving no reply the troops sat and waited. It is now known that there were more troops resting at Y beach than there were Turkish troops defending the landings at X, W and V beaches.

During the evening and into the night, the Turks attacked the forces at Y beach. At dawn they withdrew but then made a final assault and broke through the centre of the British line (helped by some of the naval shells falling amongst Allied troops). The attack was stopped and the Turks withdrew again. However the British forces were said to be completely panic-stricken and one lieutenant signalled to a ship to send boats for his men to be evacuated. The sight of men leaving the beach signalled to everyone else that they were to evacuate, and so they did with no one to stop them. The Colonel in charge was unaware of his troops leaving until he had no reply to his messages for help at the frontline. When he realised that they had gone, he gave up too and left. This has since been described as one of the most disgraceful episodes in the history of the British Army.

On S beach the situation was similar. The troops landed and the entire position was taken by 8am. From the high ground where they were, V beach was clear to see as was X beach. Despite this the British forces dug in and stayed put. Again the excuse for inaction was that they were following instructions and waiting for the troops from X, W and V beaches to advance.

At X beach there were only 12 Turkish troops and the landing was relatively easy. At 8am the British forces began to move forward as planned. One company encountered Turkish forces after around 800 yards and attacked and took Hill 141. Another group going in a different direction encountered Turkish forces at 500 yards. By 11:30am seven British companies were engaged in fighting around one and a half companies of Turkish troops. However as more troops landed on the beach, they were not brought into the battle but remained on the beach instead, doing nothing in particular.

This is thought to have been due to the heavy losses of commanding officers. At 6pm the general in command on the beach telegraphed for instructions and at 8pm he was told to remain on the beach for the night. The troops dug in, in a semicircle 800 yards from the beach.

W and V beaches were chosen as the main landing beaches for British forces. As such the navy had shelled them on many occasions prior to the landings and this alerted the Turks to their importance. These beaches were therefore very well defended with lines of wire, trip wires in the sea and trenches all around.

The 1st Battalion of the Lancashire Fusiliers landed on W beach, and due to the gentle slope of the beach, it was also intended to land all the heavy equipment and guns there. The initial naval bombardment in the morning had no effect on the wire on the beaches and did not take out any Turkish troops or guns. The Turkish forces waited until the boats reached the beach before opening fire. The boat containing all four British machine guns grounded in very deep water and three of the guns were lost.

Brigadier-General Hare noticed a gap between the north end of the wire and the cliffs, so he led two platoons through. Once through they managed to occupy some undefended trenches and found themselves behind the Turks, who were firing at the British troops as they landed. The Turks were immediately shot.

Another company at the other end of the beach also found a way through the wire and by 7:15am the beach was relatively safe from Turkish fire. Again, Allied troops came under fire from shells from the navy offshore. The maps were inadequate; the attack organised against the fort on Hill 138 actually took place on a completely different hill.

Once the beaches and surrounding areas were captured, the officers in charge awaited their orders but in the meantime dug in. In the analysis of the failures on Gallipoli, the lack of initiative on the part of those commanding the British forces is criticised again and again. They had meticulous orders, which were followed but once the targets were accomplished they waited for fresh orders, which were slow in coming. This was not an issue for the Turkish forces.

V beach has been described as like a stage or an amphitheatre with a semi-circular mound for seating around 500 yards behind the beach. Here the Turks set up their guns to fire on the stage. Lieutenant Patton, in his report on the landings, said that 'Truly a more unpromising site for a landing could scarcely be imagined'.

The British thought that the naval shelling would clear the beach of wire and destroy the Turkish guns. It did neither. Again the Turks waited until the first boats reached the shore before opening fire. Many men were killed in their boats, others jumped into the sea and, weighted down with their equipment, they were drowned. It is said in the Turkish accounts that none of the first waves of boats were able to return to the ships to collect more troops.

The *River Clyde*, the 'Trojan horse' packed with 2,000 troops ran aground as planned but the boats that were to bridge the gap to the shore went adrift. The heroic efforts of the men who jumped into the sea, and worked to form a bridge for the troops to get ashore, led to the awarding of six V.C.s. When the gap was finally bridged, men ran down the sides of the ship only to be shot and killed. General Hunter-Weston had no idea of the carnage and sent a signal from his command centre on a battleship offshore telling the troops on the *River Clyde* to land. Another attempt was made with many more deaths. Poor communications meant that he continued to signal all morning until he was eventually told about the situation at 2:30pm. In the first wave many officers were killed.

At 8:30am they mistakenly believed that the landings at X, W and V beaches had been successful, and so orders were given for the main force to land. Those landing at V beach soon encountered the boatloads of the dead and heard the messages shouted from those on the *River Clyde* not to land. Many more died. After dark, the remaining troops on the *River Clyde* went ashore under the cover of darkness to join those who had made it to the cover of a sandbank. Meanwhile, the Turkish forces were reinforced in the area and one of the orders was indeed to 'drive the enemy into the sea'.

The next day the attack on V beach started again. The Turks still had machine guns covering the middle of the beach, and a path was needed through the wire that was fastened to tall posts in lines across the beach. Corporal Cosgrove of the Royal Munster Fusiliers, described as an Irish Giant ran forwards and began clearing a way through, wrenching the posts out of the ground. It was said to have been an incredible sight. At last a gap was made and the Turkish trenches were charged and taken. Corporal Cosgrove was awarded the V.C. V beach was eventually secured by around 3pm on the 26th April.

Diaries from the soldiers who landed talk about no rifle covers being provided, despite being requested. This meant that after a good soaking in sea water, some soldiers had to get out brushes and oil and clean their rifles on the beaches before they could fire, whilst they were under heavy fire themselves. The lack of waterproof canisters also meant that food rations were soaked in salt water and were inedible, maps were wet and binoculars and compasses became useless. Poor planning also led to poor medical care for the men who were injured and for those needing evacuation.

In the build up to the Second World War, Lt Colonel G.S. Patton (later to become General Patton) was commissioned 'to examine the methods used in the defence against the landing operations as illustrated by the Turkish defence of Gallipoli'. His report was to be important in the successful planning of the D-Day landings in Normandy in 1944. The lessons he cites for the failure of the initial landings on Gallipoli were not just the bravery and organisation of the Turkish forces but also:

- The disadvantage of the slow British operations in preparing for the landings, which only served to warn the enemy.
- The tendency of the British not to push on after an initial success.
- The total inability of ships to destroy land forts.

Patton also commented on the vital importance of an advance base without which no landing operation can ever be successful. He describes the British as 'blessed with an amazing lack of forceful leadership while on the other hand, the Turks in all moments of crisis, possessed leaders of admirable force'. The failings in the British military leadership were to lead to more disasters on the Peninsula and the eventual evacuation.

Signals and Communications on Gallipoli: I Volunteer for a Dangerous Mission

Soon after landing, we were required to establish communications. We landed the horses from a barge to the shore, gathered our equipment and drew up to the Headquarters of the 29th Division under what became known as Hunter-Weston Hill (Hill 138). Immediately we got busy running out cable lines. Unfortunately, we were exactly like a Battery of Artillery in appearance, and so were shelled all the time we worked. This meant casualties in both men and horses, so that we could not use the horses as much as was necessary, and soon we gave up using them altogether.

Shelling became heavier and more frequent but we had to work on. Somehow we had to put the noise and any fear that we may have had out of our minds to concentrate on our signals work.

It didn't take long for us to realise that horses were not suited to this type of warfare. In the Boer War, Officers sat on horses above the fighting to observe the battle but this was very different. Here the horse lines stood out above ground and were clear targets. We were in dugouts ourselves. The shells came from Achi Baba Hill to our front and the big stuff from the Asiatic coast to our right. Horses could not fall flat as we did when a shell came over and so were very vulnerable. This was perhaps the most difficult thing to cope with – seeing the horses tremble and hearing them whimper as the shells fell around them.

We tried to use our wagons to lay the cables but were constantly seen and under fire with the result that all our training to put lines out at speed was wasted. We needed armoured vehicles, not horses. We had to revert to laying lines using hand-barrows or small drums carried on our backs. Trench warfare was clearly new to the Army.

The Fleet initially depended on flags, Morse code, semaphore or mirrors and lamps. General HQ was first on a ship then a neighbouring island, Imbros. To overcome the communications problems, eventually, a submarine cable had to be provided and a ship was run ashore at W beach to form a pier. It was necessary to have some communication with the shore from the pier, so a line was to be fixed from the top of the ship's mast and made fast to a point on the cliff top ashore, then on to General HQ Signal Office.

I was chosen to do the job, probably because I was athletic and because I always put my name forward for any new venture. The job entailed climbing the last 20 feet of mast with a line (D5) cable fastened to my belt. Then, on arriving at the top, fastening myself around the mast, releasing the telephone cable from the back of my belt, taking it round the mast in two or more turns to prevent it sliding down, then fastening it securely and passing the loose end down to clear the crow's nest below to be pulled up to the cliff. Pulling the cable up to the cliff top and attaching it to a large stake in the ground was not an easy task, and it took several men. I looked up at the mast with the wire fastened in my belt. It didn't look too difficult. Then I climbed the rigging to the crow's nest, so far so good, but I was surprised at the thickness of the mast. From below this looked climbable. I tested it with climbers. It was too hard and resisted the spurs. There was only one way and that was the hard way, so slowly up I went.

The weight of the wire in my belt increased. At last I reached the cap at the top of the mast. Then I had the difficult job of passing the wire round the mast and making off. I looked down. The deck did look small and narrow. I could see the seabed clearly, and the rocks at the bottom. I thought that if I fell I would try and miss the deck by jumping for the water. Luckily, everything turned out well and I came down. In the meantime, the other boys had been fixing a telephone on the ship and when the shore party got to the Signal Office we were through.

I was a Linesman attached to the main Signal Office at Cape Helles, responsible for laying and maintaining the communication lines, which were ground cables radiating to various company headquarters.

We had to run out an attack line, a special telephone line, which ran from Corps Headquarters to a sap (a narrow trench dug at a right angle to the existing line) in front of the front line in a position where the battle could be observed during its course. It was specially chosen. The messages were routine: 'Our Infantry are attacking J14' (the trenches were lettered and numbered because they were so numerous); 'Our Infantry have captured J14 and consolidating' (that meant turning the fire step round); 'Our Infantry are attacking J15'; 'Our Infantry have captured J15'; 'Enemy counter-attack on J15'; 'Enemy have retaken J15' and so it went on. At the end of the day, we might have captured one or we might have lost one, we hardly seemed to be making any progress.

The observation posts for the Commander were specially prepared because the top brass would be observing, particularly the General in charge of the attack. The Commander-In-Chief, General Hamilton, observed from there with his aides.

The line was laid in duplicate or as a ladder or it might be a circle so that if broken by shell fire, only half was lost. It was laid on the surface although the ground was difficult with trenches everywhere and, naturally, it had to be laid at night because we had to work above ground, out of the trenches. During the day we would have been under constant observation which, in those parts, meant certain death. The man who laid it was also responsible for maintaining the cable during the battle, presumably because he knew where it was and it would be an incentive to him to make it as safe as possible.

When the attack began, there was almost a continuous rain of bullets, this being a feature of the Gallipoli fighting. The observers of the battle were protected as much as possible, they looked through Naval range finders[9] that had two lenses, one at each end of a bar, and in front of them they had a large steel shield and sandbags.

When the battle was busy the man who had laid the line, a signaller like me, would think: 'I hope the line does not get hit, there will not be much chance out there if I have to get out'.

---

[9]　See picture here: http://www.museumoftechnology.org.uk/militaria.php?cab=optics

The rain of bullets was like hail. It felt awfully naked out there, all alone with not a face to be seen. Then suddenly it happened. The line was 'Dis'. Perish the thought. Try another line, plug in another phone – it worked! Ah, faulty phone, must repair it. Open the case, a wire disconnected. Put back. Base closed. Tried on line. Worked. What a relief.

The battle died away. It was time to look around. The Generals stood down so, on one occasion, I looked out. The ground in front was covered with bodies, everywhere some in lines, some alone, on some a limb moved. An ambulance man appeared. He had Red Cross armbands. Another appeared with a stretcher. They lent over one body and rolled him on to the stretcher, then lifted him and went back to the trench.

Suddenly, as I watched, a line of men appeared from the enemy trenches, led by an Officer in front with a drawn sword. They came on across the ground between live trenches. I called out to the Artillery General and he sprang to the telephone. Immediately, he gave an order to a Battery and soon shells were bursting among them. They faltered and fell and the attack died away, leaving more bodies on the ground.

The battle continued all day without us gaining any trenches. There were, however, a lot of casualties.

Over on the left flank in front of the wadi the two front lines, ours and theirs, were only a few yards apart and there was no barbed wire. Indeed, none could be put out we were so close together. When bombs were first made, they looked and felt like jam tins (which is what we called them). You could just throw the bombs across into the Turkish trenches in this part of the line. The ground between the lines received all the rubbish thrown out by both armies.

So here was the most dangerous part of our line because raids were frequent. I was given the job of running out the attack line. This had to be carefully laid from the Division Headquarters to a selected spot in the front line, from where there was a useful view of the battle and the Commanders could see the action and give orders as the battle progressed. On this occasion, I was running the telephone line along part of the trench where it was pegged down under the fire step, that being the safest part against breakages.

On this day, two of us were bending down to fasten the line when there was a shout. Still bending, I looked up to see a man with a bayonet preparing to jump from the parapet on top of me. I didn't have time to turn and shoot. Instinctively, I moved to one side and braced myself. He yelled out as he jumped into the trench – I waited for him to fall on me. Then I heard a thud and turned to face him. Fortunately for me as he landed he fell backwards landing on his bottom and dropping his rifle and bayonet. His companion, who was threatening my comrade, did exactly the same thing so the Infantry boys seized them as prisoners.

I had to sit there for a few minutes to recover my poise. I thanked the Infantry boys for their help. The attack was just a limited effort, and had been intended to seize a few prisoners to be used for information on the coming battles. Had they in fact seized me, they would have had a real prize for we were told what the attack line would be expected to achieve and how the movements were effected so that we could keep the Commanders in communication with General HQ.

Signals and Communications in the First World War

General Hamilton praised the contribution of the Signals Service on Gallipoli, recognising the difficulties they worked within. In his dispatch of 26th August 1915 he recorded[10]:

> The working of the telegraphs and telephones and the repair of lines often under heavy fire, has been beyond praise. Casualties have been unusually high, but the best traditions of the Corps of Royal Engineers have inspired the whole of their work. As an instance, the central telegraph office at Cape Helles (a dugout) was recently struck by a high explosive shell. The officer on duty and twelve other ranks were killed or wounded and the office entirely demolished, but No. 72003 Corporal G.A.Walker, Royal Engineers, although much shaken, repaired the damage, collected the men, and within 39 minutes re-opened communication by apologising for the incident and by saying he required no assistance.

---

[10] National Archive CAB/45/230 *Signals – Gallipoli*; account furnished by Major H.C.B. Weymss, DSO, MC, R.Signals.

Communications in 1915 were a world away from how we communicate today. An efficient communications system was imperative for military success and a range of different methods were used. These included: runners, (message carriers such as despatch riders and men in small boats), carrier pigeons and visual signalling. The telegraph and telephone were used when positions were more permanent, such as in the trenches. Wireless communication was relatively new and grew in its use during the war particularly in the Middle East but more about that later.

Communicating with the Navy during the landings

The landings on Gallipoli were the first time that the navy and the Army had been required to work closely together. Before the landings they had each used different systems of communication so it was important that these were brought together before the landings. General Hamilton appointed to the post of Director of Signals a man who had experience of both the navy and the army, Lieutenant Colonel Bowman-Manifold. Knowing the differences, he issued a pamphlet to all units taking part in the landings entitled *Signal Organization for Combined Operations*. In one example the Army adopted the navy's use of the 24 hour clock.

Unfortunately there was insufficient time for signallers to become completely familiar with the new signalling arrangements before the landings, and difficulties inevitably arose. For example, Army operators were not familiar with naval ciphering codes so delays occurred in transmitting messages from the shore to ship and back because messages had to be ciphered and deciphered at each end.

During the landings the navy were responsible for ship to ship and ship to shore communications. They used visual communications, landing small signal parties on each beach. Signalling under fire was a dangerous job since the men were obvious targets, so many small boats were needed to ferry messages. A shortage of these small boats caused problems – Hamilton described in his diary the trouble he had getting in touch with the army on shore when he was on a boat and using the naval communication system.

The life of a Linesman

The army took charge of all on-shore communications on Gallipoli, laying telephone lines to connect the various army headquarters to the beach signals offices. Telephone lines were often cut by exploding shells and the signallers had to run out to repair the lines. They found it hard to lay lines across the difficult terrain too. After the landings, when the troops dug in, cables were buried but not sufficiently deep to avoid all shell damage. Regularly, during battles, the signallers were sent out under fire to repair the lines.

As with all other equipment, there was a shortage of signalling equipment throughout the war. Improvisation was the order of the day with telephone receiver diaphragms being made out of tobacco tin lids. There was also a shortage of signallers, so they had to be moved around between units to cover.

Visual Signalling

Visual signals were relayed from shore to ship and back by signallers in a variety of ways. If available heliographs were used during the day, when the weather permitted, and electric lamps were used at night. Heliographs signal by flashes of sunlight reflected from a mirror – the flashes are produced by briefly tilting the mirror, or by interrupting the beam with a shutter. Flag semaphore was also used.

Telephones and Telegraph

Telegraph was the established method of communication in the Army when the war began in 1914, with lines of communication emanating from the War Office to the command centres in France and the Middle East via underwater cables. Messages were sent using Morse code.

Telephones became more popular as the war progressed however the original ones were not very popular. They could be used for speaking over short distances but often had to be used as 'buzzer phones' whereby the officer dictated a message to a signaller who buzzed it through using Morse code to another signaller who translated it back to his officer. Secrecy was a problem with the telephone, due to the possibility of enemy interception by tapping into the wire. This was not a problem with the telegraph since multiple messages were being sent down the wire at the same time.

Behind the front line, where the troops were dug into trenches, cables and wires were used to connect different headquarters. Some cables were buried or ran along the ground and others were set up poles (known as 'airline'). In the trenches, the cables were always susceptible to shell damage, and in France they were dug deeper and deeper as the war went on. As soon as the troops began to advance, signalling reverted to visual methods and to message carriers. In Mesopotamia and Palestine the distances were greater and often message carriers were killed en route, and even when they did arrive the information was usually out of date and could not to be relied upon for making decisions in the middle of the fighting.

Troops in the Middle East were more mobile than in France, moving forward on a regular basis, and distances were significant. Some cables needed to stretch over hundreds of miles. Finding faults and making repairs over these distances was time consuming, and the lines were prone to damage by local people. In any area of the war the local telegraph and telephone networks were commandeered for use by the army as they advanced, so it was not always necessary to install new equipment.

Wireless

Wireless technology was in its infancy at the start of the war. Wireless sets were large and heavy, some weighed over a ton and needed masts rising to over 80 feet (24 metres). Masts of this height were not suitable to trench war as in France but could be used in the Middle East where cables in the desert were problematic. British forces in Mesopotamia used wireless as the only means of communication since the sets could send and receive messages over a distance of up to 350 miles.

Wireless was also used in Gallipoli for ship to shore communication but the main form of communication on Gallipoli remained by cable with underwater cables laid to connect the Peninsula with General Headquarters (GHQ) on Imbros and on to Egypt.

In Palestine the British realised they could intercept Turkish wireless communications, so they began to systematically destroy any telephone or telegraph lines to force the Turks to use only wireless. Since they could intercept the Turkish wireless system, the British thought that their own system would be intercepted too, so reduced its use and installed more cables. It was also the case that the climate in Egypt and Palestine caused more interference to wireless communications, making it less reliable compared to fixed cable communications.

Shambolic Conditions

The planning for the landings seemed inept right from the start. Being in GHQ Signals, we knew some of what was going on, and of the plans, since we passed the messages along the lines and listened in to check the communications were working. It soon became obvious to us that the Commander-in-Chief, Hamilton, had no experience of landing troops anywhere on a hostile shore and, more importantly, he had not visualised his plan of Campaign together with the total requirements needed. Winston Churchill, who originated the plan, never rose above the position of Captain in a Cavalry Regiment, so his experience of an amphibious landing wasn't much either, and the home planners under Kitchener were fully occupied with the Campaign in France. France took priority. This lack of planning affected us from the outset.

Once ashore we did not have the necessities of war. There was no supply ammunition to the fighting troops when we landed. We had to sustain ourselves by taking all from the comrades killed and wounded. It was terrible taking from the dead but we had no choice.

Neither did we have the right guns. The idea was prevalent that the navy could support the landings, so no effort was made for land Artillery except the 12-pounder Horse Artillery and the 18-pounders of the Field Batteries, which fired a lot of useless shrapnel. Only one Battery of Howitzers was sent, and their guns were from the Boer War. One 60-pounder Battery of two guns was the big gun but they were field not Howitzer, and useless in trench warfare. In any case, they had little ammunition. They were reduced to 10 rounds on occasions before they could open up.

It was clear that no plans had been made for a long Campaign on the Peninsula. If they had planned for us to be here for some time then they would have thought of establishing a pier head or supply position at the outset.

Throughout our time on Gallipoli, we didn't have any fresh water – and the water we had was never enough to quench our thirst. In fact there was no fresh water source on the Peninsula since all the wells and springs were soon empty or contaminated, so it all had to be brought ashore by boat. It was one of, if not *the* most precious commodity on Gallipoli, particularly in the hot summer. Supplies, at first, were put ashore by the Fleet; this was seawater, condensed by the battleships. Later it was shipped in barges from Egypt, Greece and the islands. But supplies were quite inadequate, and all the time we were thirsty. Not surprisingly, we carefully protected any water we had.

In the early days one pint per day was the usual ration, quite insufficient for anyone working hard, especially in the dust, sand and heat. This was for all purposes and as the cook required it for making tea, we had none ourselves for the first three months. It all had to be purified. Chloride of lime was used for this purpose, which made everything taste very strange. When we were given a water bottle the ration could, in fact, be drunk at one go, it was nothing. Landing soldiers on a peninsula in the heat of summer in an area with no fresh water and such poor supplies shipped from the local islands was just bad planning. We were always thirsty, which we never got used to, and we had no water for washing ourselves.

With no water it was impossible to clean things such as mess tins and other eating equipment. Everything was eaten out of the same tin and so gradually the flavours merged into one – stew, soup, tea, porridge all tasted the same with the added ingredient of chlorine.

Even when the water was brought from Greece in barges, our ration was never increased much because more and more troops came ashore to join the battles so what we had, then had to go further. It was quite laughable to see new units arrive with large water tanks that they parked near their cookhouses. We knew they would never be filled because water was measured in dixies (our small mess tins).

About three months after the landings, we found that the Divisional Headquarters of the 29th Division had a water cart with some in it, so one night four of us collected a few water bottles and went to get some. We couldn't see why the General, Hunter-Western, should have as much as he wanted while we had none. A Sentry with fixed bayonet walked up and down the area and the Guard Room was not far away. So it was decided that only two of us would carry the bottles and the others would keep watch. Jones and I crawled up to the back of the water wagon with the bottles slung around us. We lay for a moment under the pipe at the back with the taps on it. Then, carefully I put one bottle under the tap and Jones turned it on. There was a loud 'plop' as the water hit the bottom of the bottle but we lay quiet. We filled that one and tried another. The second 'plop' aroused the Sentry and he came round the vehicle with his bayonet ready for action, so we rolled under the wagon, out of the front and ran. We had one bottle, not much and the risk was too great so we never tried that source again.

The days were hot. Then in September it rained and we were flooded! In fact the climate on Gallipoli went from extreme heat to extreme cold. Many of us suffered from sunburn, particularly the wounded as they lay between the trenches or on the beaches awaiting evacuation. The heat caused all sorts of intestinal complaints; the dust caused respiratory problems; and when the cold came in November there were 16,000 admissions for frostbite and exposure. The water question was never solved, only eased a little. All the time we were on shore we were short.

Food supplies were equally poor. For the first three months our food included hard tack biscuits, six per day because of the absence of baking. These biscuits, according to the tins, had been made in 1902, sealed and put in store. Many were absolutely riddled with weevils, dead in the tins, but we had to share them out and eat them for there was nothing else. It was three months before a field bakery was started. Then we were allowed a one-pound loaf, later reduced by two slices!

Butter came in tins, which was a good job because when on the ships it was runny and when ashore in the A.S.C. depots it was liquid and often rancid. Cheese arrived in a semi-soft state. A whole cheese put on the ground immediately assumed a different shape. It was warmed up as it came from England in ships, then our climate warmed it further. There had clearly been no forethought. We were operating in a hot climate with no way of keeping food cool. Shipping butter and cheese to troops in these conditions was stupid. What did they feed their troops in the Boer War I wondered – butter from England?

Meat at first was absent. Then we had corned beef bully, one tin to five men. Sometimes, we had Maconochie rations, a whole meal in a tin, which we punched two holes in and warmed it up. This was a sure dysentery maker but it was hard not to eat it since there was little else.

The Maconochie Brothers of Aberdeen were contracted to produce the meat and vegetable rations. A tin of Maconochie was a stew of turnips, carrots, potatoes and meat. The label on the tin said it could be eaten hot or cold. To eat it hot the can had to be put in boiling water for 30 minutes which was usually impossible on Gallipoli, so we often ate it cold and hated it.

Flies were everywhere, in their millions. If a cook left a dish of food standing, the lid was immediately covered with flies, many working their way inside, polluting the food. It was a common sight to see a man eating and waving arms and his food about to keep the flies off.

Jam was a regular issue. We used more than we ate for the fly traps. It was made by the Tickler's factory in Grimsby. We hated the marmalade because it tasted of turpentine, but we had to continue to draw it as ration. It was offered again and again. At first we stored it, then used it on the fly traps but when it rained and the trenches and dugouts were flooded it became useful. The floors became a wet, sticky, muddy mess so we began to pave them with the only firm objects we had, namely Tickler's marmalade and bully beef tins (full). I found out later that they used turnips and swedes as puree to add bulk to the fruit and thicken the jam.

Sugar was plentiful, and while England was without tea and cocoa we had enough for everyone. It was the variety that palled. After all, our cooks were amateurs – normally the men who were not so good at other jobs got relegated to the cookhouse. Mostly it was stew and tea.

Neither Hamilton, our Commander-In-Chief, nor any of his staff ever thought the men would want a drink of beer, a glass of wine or a bottle of whisky. Indeed, Hamilton said he was teetotal and everyone else ought to be. He ought really to have been a parson. Probably, he would have made a better one than a soldier! Some of our men swapped things with the French to obtain red wine – thin stuff that they referred to as vin baptisme because of the apparent lack of alcohol in it. And there was no tobacco either. I had smoked Woodbines before the war.

Some wooden hearts needed softening and, eventually, some Greeks arrived on the beach bringing huts. They erected them near the beach, selling strings of figs and chocolates. That was all they were allowed to sell. We were pleased to see them, even though they sold poor quality fare. We had little money anyway since there was no regularity in paying wages. It was only now and again that we received anything. In our circumstances, alcohol would have been a good thing, to sterilise things and perhaps stave off some of the illnesses such as dysentery. We had nearly every stomach complaint going.

Jealousy Over a Fly Trap

Flies literally bred in millions. A wounded man picked up after a battle would be covered with them, and they contaminated his wounds. Bodies of our dead were left to rot on the surface, decomposing and attracting flies. Incredible that there were no plans to remove our dead and deal with them in a dignified manner. The horses suffered too, and many wounds were infected. A horse, poor thing, might have a sore but before long the flies would make it into a hole deep into its body. There were hundreds of dead horses lying on the beaches, all killed by shell fire and thrown over the cliffs in the hope that the sea would take them. It didn't and flies had a birthday.

Flies carried all sorts of diseases, and inevitably Battalions 'in rest' lost more men than were killed in the fighting. They seemed to have learned nothing from Florence Nightingale and the Crimea, and it wasn't that far away from where we were fighting.

With the lack of water and the inability to clean anything combined with the flies and dust, it was inevitable that there would be illness. Infections and dysentery affected everyone from the Generals to us frontline troops.

I don't know how many men were sick whilst on Gallipoli, but later I heard that a doctor suggested that the effects of diarrhoea and dysentery were one of the main causes of the failure of the Campaign.

Various contraptions were made to catch the flies. One such was a framework about three feet six inches wide and six feet high with rollers top and bottom covered in material to wind round the rollers. It looked like a giant towel roller. Anything we had that was sweet and would attract the flies was put on the material. Under the bottom roller there was a scraper. When the material was covered in flies, the roller would be turned and the scraper at the bottom would scrape the flies into a heap underneath. At the end of a day the piles of dead flies were shovelled up and put in the incinerator (we had progressed by then) with the horse manure. In one day, one of these caught a sackful of flies; the numbers did not decrease though, until the frost came. We were continually tortured by them.

One of our boys had a Japanese fly trap sent from home. It was a smaller device than the contraptions we made. It worked from a clock spring turning the roller to catch and kill the flies. It was good and caught them in their hundreds, we were all very envious of him!

Post From Home

Even postal arrangements were missing. We all wanted to hear news from home, something to bring some happiness into that miserable place. We were young and hadn't been away from our families before for this length of time, and not hearing from them was hard. After some time a ship brought mail, landing it in a huge pile, but no arrangement for delivery to our Units was ever made. Searchers for our Units walked all over the pile, throwing bags here and there. Parcels were often lost or broken up. Later letters and parcels were two or three months arriving. We often talked in the dugouts about what we could do to improve matters; the poor postal system and the lack of food and water affected us all.

When parcels did come from home, they were shared. What did I get in the parcels from home? I can't remember but I do know that Mother sent things as often as she could. I remember the happiness I felt when letters arrived with stories from home.

There was genuine camaraderie between us soldiers and a mutual desire to help each other. Often we benefited as so many casualties were not there to receive their parcels. These were shared between us too, and I remember one mother continued to send parcels even after her boy was killed, asking us to share them.

In the end we had one green envelope to write home once a month. Rigid instructions were issued on what you couldn't say to fathers and mothers. Censorship by Officers was deliberate and keen. We did not like our Officers reading the details we gave as news to our families. Many times they exorcised what was said although it was true.

Humour in the Latrines

I'm sorry to mention this but the latrines that the Army provided were primitive, just a trench with a pole across the top, open all the time to flies. There was no privacy at first, nothing in the way of a curtain, which I found very difficult to begin with. I was just eighteen and had been brought up to have good manners and to respect privacy and dignity but it didn't take long to lose my inhibitions, we all got used to it after a while, we had to.

There was humour in the latrines, especially when a shell burst immediately in front of those sitting on the bar and they all fell backwards into it. They had to go down to the sea to be washed and we laughed at them. Luckily it never happened to me!

Macabre

The smell of death was everywhere – a pervading, sickly smell that was not entirely objectionable except in large doses.

In the nine months that we were on Gallipoli, there were 252,000 casualties out of the 489,000 men sent to fight, roughly 28,000 per month. Of these around 56,000 died. I read later that the numbers of Turks fighting who became casualties were almost identical but their dead were said to number more at around 86,000.

The Naval Division occupied part of the centre of the line with the French troops on their right. They had a lot of casualties and the ground in some parts was piled with bodies, some had been partially buried by shells. One of these was at the crossroads that ran up to the front line. On the left were the English Headquarters, and on the right the French. There was a man buried just by the crossroad and he had an arm sticking up out of the ground. In his hand someone had put the sign 'Division HQ' with an arrow pointing the way. This is just an example of how cheap life became when no man knew when he would go. It was macabre.

The War Graves Commission was not established then and men were expendable. General Headquarters had no organisation for burying the dead and, apparently, it was nobody's job to see to it. Only when the smell became a nuisance were they buried. Some of the dead were burned but mostly they were just put in old trenches and covered in, otherwise they stayed on top rotting everywhere. The Generals were still trying to plan battles at Waterloo. They hadn't caught up.

The whole Campaign really was a picture of muddle and incompetence. The military planning for the landings clearly was based on the presumption that we would march straight on to take Constantinople with no opposition and they, the Generals and Admirals, would sail round to meet us. Those in charge at GHQ and Divisional Headquarters really had no idea of how to run the Campaign. They were all regular soldiers whose career had always been in the Army and, frankly, we all thought they were mostly brainless. My comrades in the Territorial's had all had careers at home, and often could see what was needed. So, as time went by, we began to despise those in charge. They were just eleven, brainless, loud noises, only fit to shout orders on parades when dressed in fancy uniforms cleaned by their Batmen[11]. In battle, yes, they were not cowards and went over the top with alacrity, but fell down on organisation badly. Most of them had no technical training and little fancy for it.

Everywhere there were dead bodies. That was why diseases of every kind were rampant. Dysentery and enteric fever (typhoid) caught the solders in thousands. Indeed, I should say every man had dysentery, died or went into hospital. Very few managed to cure themselves. Doctors had no cure for these diseases but there were few doctors in the Army in those days. Those doctors

---

[11]   An officer's servant.

who were there relied upon a pill, the venerable Number 9. I've no idea what it was, probably just a sugar pill. When we could get it, usually in parcels from home, we took Collis Browne's mixture – that worked best. The ingredients were a mixture of laudanum (a solution of opium), cannabis, and chloroform – not surprisingly it also relieved our pain, especially toothache!

Our Army biscuits were as hard as nails. They should have been soaked in tea or water to soften them but we had no water, so soldiers regularly broke their teeth on them. This created a problem since there were no dentists and the men had to be evacuated for dental treatment, which meant that they were away for weeks. Since they were needed, many men were denied the opportunity for treatment and had to live with their toothache for months. Sometimes we helped if the Regimental Medical Officer wouldn't pull the tooth.

Medical services were not well planned for the landings or for the Campaign as a whole. We could tell that there was a shortage of medical staff to deal with the enormous number of casualties.

Soldiers with minor ailments were kept on Gallipoli due to the need to have sufficient men to fight. The definition of a 'minor ailment' varied according to the needs of the Generals in the forthcoming attacks.

Throughout our time on the Peninsula we looked out for each other, after all we were all in this together. When one of us was injured we all helped, doing what was necessary to get our comrades to the nearest casualty station. Soon after the landings and near where we were working to set up communications, hundreds of injured men lay on the beach waiting to be collected and taken to the hospital ships. What a terrible sight – all those brave men lying there in full sun, in the heat of the day with sand and dirt blowing into their wounds as the shells landing on the beach threw it up.

The Medical Services on Gallipoli

During a battle priority was given to moving troop reinforcements forward, consequently the wounded had to wait before they were moved back to the regimental aid post. This meant that the wounded often waited a considerable time, as the trenches were narrow and even stretcher bearers had trouble moving through them. The French got around this by digging separate trenches to move the wounded.

At the start of the campaign there was a shortage of stretchers, so blankets and coats were used with rifles or sticks for handles. The wounded were taken by the stretcher bearers to the regimental aid post just behind the front line, where they were assessed and given drugs and dressings. Their name, rank and number would be recorded and they would be given a label saying what their wounds were and what treatment had been given. From there they would be carried to an Advanced Dressing Station and then on to the Casualty Clearing Station, usually on the beach.

At the Casualty Clearing Station wounds were assessed, and if necessary emergency operations were performed. The men were sorted according to the degree of their injuries, and they would then wait to be evacuated onto a hospital ship. There were usually long waits to be evacuated, and with the flies and dirt many wounds became infected. The history books say that many infections and amputations would have been avoided if the logistics for dealing with the casualties had been better. Indeed the medical arrangements for the wounded on Gallipoli have been described by historians as a 'nightmare'.

Soldiers on stretchers were winched onto the hospital ships using a steam winch. This could take some time, particularly if the weather was bad or if there was a high wind. Casualties were also hit by shells and bullets. The ships were of varying sizes, some were passenger liners that could take over 4,000 patients. Official hospital ships were white and were protected under the Geneva Convention from attack. 'Black' ships were also used to take casualties but since they carried supplies they were vulnerable to attack.

Once on board treatment was administered as far as possible, depending on the sea conditions. Some casualties were taken to Mudros, a four hour journey in good weather. Some went directly to Egypt where the main hospital base was. This journey took just over 3 days. In Egypt, only 3,500 beds were available at the beginning of April 1915 but this soon rose to 36,000. Malta was also used, which was a journey of 5 or 6 days. A smaller hospital base was provided on Gibraltar, a further 8 days away from Malta. Some casualties were taken back to England – a journey that today takes 2 weeks by sea. The ANZAC troops who were seriously injured were taken back to Australia and New Zealand, a journey that today may take 6 weeks.

Records show that for one of the 1,000 bed tent hospitals in Cairo there was only 1 matron, 15 sisters and 30 staff nurses.

Hygiene & Keeping Clean

On Gallipoli, we could only keep clean when we could get down to the sea for a bathe, and W beach was always crowded. Similarly, washing clothes was impossible, so this was done in the sea too – but salty clothes were not too comfortable, especially near the skin. I wore a shirt for three months without washing it. I must have smelled but we all smelled, so no one said anything! But the sea wasn't clean – all the horses killed for a long time were taken to the cliffs and thrown over, and they floated about, decomposing and contaminating the sea where we swam. The bodies from the early landings and other deaths were not retrieved either for some time, and these also floated around contaminating the water even more.

Soon, on shore, we found ourselves covered in lice and fleas. The climate and conditions were ideal for breeding. They were everywhere in the dugouts and trenches. I remember taking off my vest and finding 19 lice in the seams. Disgusted, I made the mistake of throwing the under-vest away, not realising that it could not be replaced. My Army shirt scrubbed uncomfortably against my skin, and it got just as lousy. Everybody was in the same predicament and it was a common sight to see men wearing trousers inside out 'to give them a walk back' as they said.

We just did not know how to control the lice and the authorities were just as ignorant, although the Army surely must have endured such things in previous wars. However, they never did anything to keep the troops healthy. Apparently, when a man signed on for a shilling he was responsible for everything himself. I wish I had been told about this problem before I left for the war; I would have done some research to find the best way to deal with the pests.

I was brought up in a house of women and being clean was important to them and so to me. In my young days we were fortunate at home to have a bathroom, as most houses in those years were without, and families used tin baths or wooden washtubs. Some would use an outside washhouse where there would be a 'boiler' (this was a large metal pan with a fire of wood or coal under it). The hot water had to be ladled out into the bath. Others had a similar boiler fixed in a scullery or the kitchen. Often water had to be fetched from an outside tap or supply. Quite a number of cottages had a pump some distance away or a well in the garden. The bath in winter would be in front of the kitchen fire, in the scullery or the outside washhouse, with sacks on the stone flagged floor. Concrete was unknown in houses and outbuildings. From this, it will be obvious that in the countryside bathing was difficult for a mixed family.

In towns bathing was rather better because there were bathing establishments, Turkish baths and, generally, better water supplies, but these meant paying and it must be remembered that people were poor. They had no or very little money for extras. Families were large, heating was dear, water supplies scarce, so children followed one another in the same bath water once a week or once a fortnight, sometimes with disinfectants added for safety.

My relatives mostly lived in the country, some in villages, others on farms, so I had opportunity to see all the methods of bathing when young. Privacy was difficult, but was maintained. My first real difficulty occurred in the Army in 1914. We were in barracks in Leeds and in Bedford, then in the small town of Biggleswade, where it was possible to have a bath at the local club for six pence. So, we who could swim, swam in the river, but in the winter that was off. We were eventually billeted out into people's homes and there we used the scullery copper or iron wash boilers, often both referred to as 'The Copper'. When later we moved to billets in Southall (Bedfordshire), we used an outhouse where the family washing was done. It was a real shivering job in the winter of 1914.

In Alexandria, we swam in the sea with no difficulty. Later in Egypt, we were, fortunately, near to the Suez Canal, which I swam across hundreds of times. It was dangerous to swim in the Nile because of bilharzia, a disease that was a killer. The River Jordan was also prohibited for the same reason, but in any case, it was very dirty water on the stretch where we were by Jericho. The Dead Sea was impossible since the impurities in that were so bad that, emerging, the skin was absolutely coated with sticky salt, which needed clean water to wash it off and there wasn't much of that around. One of the small tributaries off the Jordan called the Auja was clean and fresh but we found that the Arabs were washing their mangy camels in it, so we had to 'watch it' and go upstream.

Understandably, when I came home five years later, I was determined never to miss a wash, bath, or swim and this I kept up for the rest of my life. Whenever and wherever possible I have had a bath every day and a swim too. One has only to be deprived to realise the happiness of such a facility.

At the Lancashire Landing beach we swam whenever we could. We used an aeroplane that had come down in the sea as a diving board. The wings were excellent for the purpose, being a biplane, one could dive low or high according to taste.

One day I decided to swim out to a hospital ship anchored off shore, the distance I reckoned was about a mile and it was a lovely day. Swimming out and away from the beach, the water was so clear that I could see the seabed about forty feet below. It was beautiful. With the sea lapping around my ears, covering the noise of the shelling on shore, I could dream that I was away from it all. I remember that I had the feeling of being in the air; it was a most peculiar feeling, and is something that has stayed with me.

The outward journey was very easy. I swam gently along enjoying the clear water and the relative peace and quiet of the sea (although I could still hear the sound of shells bursting every now and then). I waved to those looking at me over the ship's side and turned around to swim back. Then I knew why it had been so easy. The current was running off shore and I tried every stroke I knew on the return. At one point I wondered if I would make it, and was very glad when I could touch the bottom and stand on solid ground again. I rested before heading back to the beach. I should have remembered the strength of the current from the way it took our boat during the landings.

My father had lived and been brought up in a village without a river nearby and there had been no other facilities, so he never learnt to swim. After he drowned, my mother made sure we could all swim. My first lessons were in a reservoir used by a colliery near Cudworth. Later, in Leeds it was the principle of the city council to teach every child to swim. There were swimming baths in the town and suburbs and a lake at Roundhay.

The council employed two teachers who were designated 'Professors of Swimming'. They received the adoration of the children. Both were big, strong fellows; one had swum across the Channel and the other could swim the length of the normal bath (25 yards) in three strikes. I was in awe of them. Apart from the school times when swimming was free, the price of admission to the swimming baths was 1 penny, but on clean water days it was 2 pence, which was usually on Thursdays. The water was, of course, always clean since they used chlorine as a disinfectant but on those days the baths were emptied and filled again. The cleanest swimming baths were in Union Street in Leeds, near the markets in the middle of the town.

With the professors of swimming teaching me, I soon swam the breadth and length of the baths. The general practice was for the teacher to use a pole, which we grasped and then swam to the side. Each of us did this in turn as the teacher walked up the bath. There was also, in some baths, a suspended harness to teach the strokes. In addition to this, I went with my friends on other days to practice but mostly to enjoy ourselves; we would stay in the water all afternoon. Often we were 'turned out' when the attendant thought we had been in long enough on a Saturday afternoon, but we invariably dived in again as soon as his back was turned, so the whistle blew regularly above the shouting. Strange that baths are always constructed to maximise noise.

At the Boys Modern School, where I attended later, the baths were nearby down a short street off Cookridge Street. It was larger and broader than the standard size. One of our masters, Mr Radcliffe, acted as swimming master and, of course, by that time all the boys could swim as they mostly came from other schools. I gained all the badges for proficiency and the certificates and, for one year, the record for the longest plunge, a test open to anyone in the town. It was measured and recorded, mine being 3 quarters of a length.

The accent in my day was for strength and endurance rather than speed, although that did come into it too, for we had year-end races and competitions. I took part but was very little, being handicapped out. I was beaten by a touch, or a yard, or I gave others a length start in a two length race. When I complained, the master said it was good handicapping. It was, but not for me. I had nothing to show for it. I wanted a medal too but had to make do with knowing that I was the strongest in my year and quite possibly in the school.

The strokes we learned then were rather different from present day strokes. The breaststroke was the most used. The next was the Trudgen, the fastest. Both arms reached forward in turn, lifting and reaching, bent from the elbow, as the body turned sideways to enable you to breath under one arm. Then both arms pulled back to the sides. The leg movement was a variation of the breaststroke. Also, we had a sidestroke –the body turned sideways and one arm reached forward above the water and returned in an arch to the body while the other arm did a short forward balancing and pulling motion. The legs were used in a sort of scissor motion in unison.

There was no mixed bathing, so days and evenings were set apart for the sexes. Blenheim School near us had a girls' bath, and when we went there to give a demonstration we had to wear drawers and a dark costume. The drawers were what we called 'one leggers'. We could not touch the girls and had to use only one side of the bath, so we never had the chance to practice life saving them.

On my return home from the war I swam in Wakefield, for a time, at 7am before going to work but the bath there was dirty so I gave up until we went to Filey on holiday. In later years when we returned to Leeds, I swam at many places. I was chairman of a sports & social committee for some years, and went to the baths each week when available. There I mostly taught others and at Shaldon, near Teignmouth, I taught a young woman to swim when we were on holiday. I also taught my grandson to dive when he came to Exmouth.

I was never a high diver. I remember going to Weston-Super-Mare when the new bath opened. I climbed up onto the high platform. My, it looked a long way, but I hadn't the courage to walk down, so I dived and took all the 15 feet of water, scraped the bottom and emerged. I didn't try again!

When on ships during the war, I often looked over the side confidently and said to myself, 'If this gets torpedoed I could dive off easily, find a box to hold onto and survive' but that was in warm water.

I had many happy hours of enjoyment swimming. After the war I went holidaying in Bridlington where tents were allotted to bathers for changing in. When drying after a morning swim in a cold sea I looked down and saw that I was blue with cold. I walked into the nearest public house and had a double whisky. The next day I went swimming again and discovered the cause of my blue skin, the sun was shining through the bathing tent, which was a greenish blue – I still went and had a whisky afterwards though.

The Turkish Campaign and the Battles on Gallipoli

Until recently, little has been written about the Turkish forces and their campaign to stop the Allied invasion on Gallipoli. The Turkish forces were well trained, well fed, well equipped and well led. This was partly due to their recent fight in the Balkan Wars with Greece and Bulgaria.

Prior to the landings they had spent time building up their supplies and communication networks, and rehearsing their counterattack and defence plans. Helped by the Germans they had also fortified the coastal defences of the Dardanelles.

When it became clear that the British were mustering their forces in Egypt and a landing on Gallipoli was likely, maps of the Peninsula were drawn up by the Turkish Army Ordnance Survey section. These were accurate and were issued to battalion commanders with the order that they must not fall in to enemy hands. Anyone taking a map near the front was only allowed to carry the section of the map of the area they were in. Nevertheless, maps were captured by the Allies and sent to Egypt for copying. The British overlaid the maps with squares to help with focussing artillery fire and issued them. When the Turks captured these British maps they were impressed with the grid system and adopted it themselves.

After the landings, when both sides had effectively dug in, the Turks began a series of night attacks on the Allied trenches. For one such attack the orders simply said: 'Tonight at 10pm the entire division will attack the enemy'. During one night attack, the Turkish telephone exchange was damaged and messages about needing support to finally break through the lines did not get back to the general in charge. Not knowing the position, he ordered the Turkish forces to pull back. The night attacks were aimed particularly at the French trenches where the line was thought to be weakest but the French fought back and the night attacks reduced.

In the south at Cape Helles, British and French forces made a second attempt to capture the town of Krithia. On the 6th May 1915 they attacked with 25,000 men. It was a complete failure. The Turks held their lines and then began a big offensive to push the Anzac forces into the sea.

Wary of British aerial reconnaissance, Turkish troops marched at night towards the Anzac lines and took time to reconnoitre their routes and to rehearse their movements. During the night of the 18th/19th May over 50,000 men attacked the Anzac lines. The Australian and New Zealand forces had thought something was afoot when the routine daytime shelling reduced in the days before the attack. They knew the offensive was starting when they heard the drums and trumpets playing in the Turkish trenches. It must have been terrifying on both sides. Australian machine gun fire killed thousands of Turkish soldiers as they crossed no man's land. This, combined with the bravery and discipline of the Anzac forces, was said to have led to the failure of the assault.

Following the Anzac offensive, a temporary ceasefire was negotiated for each side to bury their dead.

At the beginning of June, the Allies made another attempt to capture Krithia. 22,000 British and 24,000 French troops launched an attack on the Turkish lines but the Turks defended well and fought back. Once again there was stalemate.

Rather than continue full on attacks, General Hamilton authorised smaller scale divisional attacks to take place to seize local targets. The French launched the first such attack at Kereves Dere on 21st June. The fighting was described as bitter but it came to nothing. On 28th June, the British attacked at Gully Ravine. This time the British had conducted aerial reconnaissance, had good maps and were well prepared. They seized the frontline Turkish trenches. Indian troops moved forward on one flank but the Turkish forces counterattacked and pushed them back.

In mid-July the British and French made a combined attack on Kereves Dere and Achi Baba, having heard rumours that the morale of the Turkish forces was low. This time the Allies went over the top and were mown down by heavy Turkish machine gun fire. The British communications system broke down during the attack due to officers being killed. This led to confusion about the progress of the battle back at divisional and brigade HQ, and when the Turks began their counterattack the Allied forces had lost the will to continue and pulled back.

Morale

The Ottoman Army had developed a replacement system for their forces based on a German system. New recruits were drafted into the army as required, and were taken to a central training base where they received full training before being sent on into specific services or for tactical training. This central supply of new but well trained troops enabled the Turkish forces on Gallipoli to be quickly replaced when casualties were high. This helped to maintain morale at the front, since the soldiers always knew help was on its way.

Morale was also maintained through other means. Living conditions were much better for the Turks than for the Allies. The Turkish soldiers lived in much more roomy dugouts, which even had electric lights. Whilst many soldiers could not read, there was nevertheless a good postal service for letters from home and newspapers were available. Divisional bands played every day, sometimes in the trenches before a battle. The regimental Imams, who often went into battle with the men, conducted regular religious services and prayers. The British reported that often they knew when there was going to be an attack because they could hear the noise building in the Turkish trenches with shouts of '*Allahu Akbar*' after the prayers.

The Turks had available to them direct supplies from Constantinople and from the surrounding countryside, coming by rail, road and ship. This meant a good supply of clean drinking water, plenty of fresh fruit and vegetables and bread baked by 'bakery platoons' delivered every day. As a result, they experienced much less sickness than the Allied forces.

Turkish troops benefited from field hospitals nearby and speedy evacuation to hospitals in Constantinople and elsewhere in the region. This led to faster treatment and more hygienic conditions than were available to the Allied forces. Another benefit open to the Turkish troops was the possibility to be taken behind the lines for rest when needed. The Allied forces were stuck on the Peninsula for the duration with only a very few being taken off to the neighbouring Greek island of Imbros for a break from the shelling.

Fortnightly Attacks:
The Death Toll Rises

Almost every fortnight we attacked the Turkish trenches, and every month a big attack was mounted. For these, telephone lines of a special kind were required to minimise any possibility of a loss of communication during the battle. There were times when Battalions and Brigade were out of communication for a whole day and no one knew what was happening in such a confused situation. In earlier wars, the Commander could ride round on his horse to find out, but trench warfare stopped that. Put your head above the trench top and you were sure to be shot at.

Hunter-Weston was in command of the 29th Division and acted as Corps General when other Divisions were brought in for an attack. I was in the Signal Office one day in 1915 when a general attack by us and the French was in progress, and when the communication lines were broken I would go out to repair them.

The battles extended the whole width of the Peninsula and the French troops were in our sight. On this day, very little progress was made as the terrain was rough and the Turks were well dug in. Also, they appeared full of confidence, perhaps because they were fighting on their own ground. The navy were providing the heavy Artillery. They stood off shore, the shells passed over our heads while the French 75's provided a somewhat regular 'pop-bang' over to our left.

When the battle had been in progress for the best part of the morning, an agitated call came through from General Cox of the 85th Brigade. He stated that a large Turkish counterattack was in progress and the French were retiring, leaving his flank exposed. What were his orders? General Hamilton quickly asked who was in support. The retiring French Colonial troops were Algerian. The flank of our troops was held by the Naval Division, who were being machine gunned heavily and they were retreating. Hunter-Weston was told that the 29th Division was in support, and without any hesitation he ordered them to fire on the retreating Naval Division, our boys. I couldn't believe my ears. The Collingwood Battalion lost 400 men killed and wounded that day, all boys who volunteered to serve in the Navy when war broke out in 1914.

The attack soon afterwards fizzled out and later I talked to some of the survivors. Apparently, when the French returned they were enfiladed,[12] and to keep their line in tact their right flank fell back to protect it from enemy infiltration. As one survivor said to me, 'We were surprised to be shot at from our boys behind'.

But it gave me the realisation of how the professional General could deliberately order the killing of his own men, with little if any thought. Hunter-Weston knew how short of men we were for this type of fighting because he was continually asking for more when there were no more to be had, yet he still gave the

---

[12] 'Enfilade' describes a military formation's exposure to enemy fire. A formation or position is 'in enfilade' if weapons fire can be directed along its longest axis.

order to kill his own. As an eighteen year-old this really was a lesson in life and death.

Pot Shots

We were working in the line one day, putting a cable under the fire step of the trench. Things were quiet. An occasional bomb came in, and the fuse could be seen so we knew how long it would go before it exploded. All or nearly all of the early bombs were homemade, filled with nails or pieces of metal, and the fuse hung out like a white cord. If it was a longish cord, we would pick it up and throw it back, or out, whichever was quickest. If it was ready to explode, a blanket would be thrown over it, which went up in the air and fell back. Once, I lobbed my overcoat over one, and when it came down it had a round hole burned in the middle of the back, but I still wore it.

One day, we came to a place where the enemy could be seen passing round a corner of his trench, and so we stopped to look. Obviously, they didn't know they could be seen until several were shot. Whenever we were passing along in our trenches we looked carefully to learn if they could see us because we were bobbing up and down with our wire, running it out and pegging it down. We made time every now and then to have a pot shot when we could see the enemy.

I remember the day that my friend, Dennison, and I were at the end of Gully Ravine. A rough track from the beach ended there and we rested on the bank on the top surveying the Peninsula and the sea all around. We looked at the Turkish trenches ahead and listened. It was a quiet day with only occasional firing in the distance and a few shells bursting here and there. The sun shone overhead and we lay on our backs looking at the sky. It seemed a long way from the war.

In Summer Gully Ravine was a dry wadi about thirty feet deep running from Achi Baba to the sea. As it ran just behind our trenches, it was used by reinforcements going into the firing line and for storing ammunition. In winter, it would be a torrent. Being so deep, it seemed safe, and a Field Battery stored their ammunition here so that when in action they could easily carry the shells up to the guns. We had to go there one day and my friend Dennison said: 'You never hear a shell that is going to hit you'. The argument about this was a constant topic on the Peninsula because the shellfire was so intense. Suddenly, there was an urgent whistle, which sounded like an approaching train in a tunnel rapidly coming near. Quickly, we threw ourselves flat under the bank of earth but the shrieking shell buried itself in the bank and did not explode. It shook dust all over us and shook us up too.

'There's your answer Dennison,' said a voice as we pushed ourselves up and dashed down the gully road, not waiting for the next shell to come over. Another three feet and we would not have known the answer. Obviously, we had been observed on our approach. We were often under enemy observation.

The Naval Observation Station

During one battle the Navy was firing heavy Artillery from the ships anchored offshore towards the Turkish trenches ahead of us. The sea all round the tip of the Peninsula was full of ships of all kinds: destroyers, battleships, transporters, and hospital ships. It was quite a picture. This was before the submarines appeared. The Turks and Germans replied fiercely as they always did for they had more ammunition than us, and the ground was dotted from time to time by bursting shells. Ahead the rattle of machine guns punctuated the usual amount of rifle fire. The sea also had its share of bursts. This carried on all morning. The messages flowed into our Signals Office about the course of the battle. Our boys were not having much success in the attacks on the enemy trenches.

I was in charge of the communication lines that day. One of these lines ran to a Naval observation station, a dugout on the cliff top above W beach where the Lancashire Fusiliers had won five Victoria Crosses for bravery during the landings in April. The sailors in the observation station sent these messages from the cliff top to the Admiral on the *Majestic*, anchored below.

Suddenly, a voice rang out 'N.O.S Lineman', that was me, 'Line Dis' – our communication line was disconnected to the Naval observation station, broken, probably damaged by a shell. I picked up a Field Telephone and hurried out into the heat of the battle to test the line. The fault was not in the vicinity so I ran along the ground looking for where it was broken, falling flat when a shell burst near and hugging the ground to avoid rifle fire. I knew that the observation station was the only link between our sea and land forces, so this was important. The line had to be repaired, and quickly.

I couldn't find a break and eventually, panting, I arrived at the observation station. A dreadful sight met my eyes. All eight men were dead. A shell had landed and burst inside the station;

it had killed everyone. They were unrecognisable. It was awful. I collected myself as far as I could, and hurriedly connected my telephone, hoping it would still be through to the Signal Office where I had come from. I held my breath and called. Yes. To my relief it was in order. Quickly, I described the position, and then a voice came on: 'Signal to the flagships. Stop Fleet bombardment. Our ships are firing into our men'. I explained I had no signalling flags with me and everything in the dugout was destroyed. The answer: 'Find some, it is very urgent, our casualties are mounting'.

I thought for a moment as I surveyed the grisly scene, 'Where oh where can I get some flags?' and I remembered that further along the cliff was a 60-pounder Battery and they would have some. I dashed along and explained my need as rapidly as I could to the Battery Commander. As Signallers we wore blue and white armbands wherever we were, and they allowed us to go anywhere without hindrance. The Battery was in action and between my panting breaths and the big guns firing he gave an order for the flags to be brought sending two of his Signallers with me, presumably to make sure my story was true.

We set up station by the dugout and I sent the message to the *Majestic*. The ships ceased firing and a boat party came ashore. They had gathered something was wrong when the station went quiet. When they saw the dugout there was silence for quite some time. Then more messages were sent describing the scene. I returned to our Signal Office and learnt that the Navy had decimated our boys with their fire and when the inevitable counterattacks came, were driven off the hill and never recaptured it.

Not long after this I was looking out to sea one morning as I came off duty at the Signal Office on Hunter-Westen Hill, which was on a rise above the top of the cliff. Out to sea there was the usual pattern of dozens of ships of all sizes: British and French navies, battleships, troopships, hospital ships, destroyers, minesweepers and lighters, all anchored and swaying on the tide. Suddenly, from the side of the *Majestic*, flagship of the Mediterranean fleet, there was a huge spout of water hurled into the air. This was higher than her mast and funnels. Then a loud explosion, and immediately she started to list. A bugle call sounded and sailors ran and stood in line at attention. Before long, she listed further and then slowly turned turtle, her green underside showing, and then she gradually sank. I watched as sailors clambered over her sides on to the upturned keel, then into the water. Meantime, other ships, alerted by the blast, lowered their boats. There were picquet boats[13], rowing boats, all around her in a very short time rescuing the sailors from the sea, all busy.

Apparently, the steel torpedo net, one of her defences, had been lifted on one side to allow the Commander to go ashore and the German submarine had used considerable skill in attack on that side as she was surrounded by other ships. The *Majestic* sank in twenty minutes with the loss of 92 lives. Not long afterwards the ships disappeared from the bay, frightened off by the German submarines.

---

[13]   Small patrol boats.

The Suffering of our Best Friends, the Horses

During the war the horses suffered terribly from rifle fire, shells and mortar. Our mounted unit left England with 76 horses but after three months we had 9 left, the others were all killed. It was heart-breaking.

There was nothing worse than hearing gunfire and going out to catch the horses as they galloped back rider-less to our lines, wounded in the head, body or legs. Their blood covered our arms as we caught them. Sadly, we shot those we could not do anything for. The average life of a horse soon after the landings was 24 hours. One day, after a bombardment, the horse standing next to Timbuc was disembowelled and cast up over Timbuc. When it dried it could not be cleaned off, so I took him down to the sea and washed him.

Things became so bad that drivers eventually took the horses to picket lines[14] tethering them together on a rope running round the base of the cliffs and there they stood each day, being brought back to the lines at night if needed. If night shelling occurred, the horses were let loose and collected the next day. As no one wanted horses in the fighting, they were never lost.

We found that two horses would not drag a dead one unless we put a hood over their heads, but so often they had to do it to collect up those that had fallen. Later we had to dig huge pits and bury the dead, and what a task it was, shooting the badly wounded. Many times the hands of those shooting shook so much that it took several bullets.

---

[14] A picket line is a rope, along which horses are tied at intervals.

It soon dawned on me that the Army should have been investing in motor vehicles instead of wasting huge resources shipping horses with their foodstuff and keepers across the world to fight. I should have known they wouldn't though, after all the Cavalry was the pride of the Army, and they were still training them to use lances and swords – they hadn't even caught up with guns! During the war I saw a heavy gun, which was stuck in the mud with 36 horses harnessed in fours trying to pull it out. The harnesses kept snapping and finally a Holt Tractor was brought to do the job. It was a demonstration, sadly one of many, of the way Kitchener and the Army High Command were still living in the era of the Crimea and Boer Wars.

Blériot flew the channel in 1909, but in 1914 we had only a few aeroplanes and the generals regarded them as toys. They wanted Battalions of men, and more men, to be used as cannon fodder, and they destroyed them in thousands, ultimately millions. A whole generation sacrificed by blockheads without two thoughts or bright ideas to rub together.

I had my first ride in a motor car in 1914. They had been growing in numbers, particularly amongst wealthy folk in Leeds. Motor vehicles were increasing in civilian life generally, but not in the Army. When I returned from the war in 1919 there had been a noticeable change with horses replaced by charabancs and the horse-drawn tramcar replaced with the electric motor. The coal cart became bags on a lorry and the delivery vehicle, a motor van. The farmers were some of the last to lose the horse because machinery was slower in coming and they grew their own fodder so it was cheaper.

The Unpopular Adjutant and the Stupid General

I was on W beach, otherwise known as Lancashire Landing when the 42nd Division were coming ashore. They were a Territorial Division that had been in Egypt from September 1914. While watching I fell into conversation with a soldier from Bury who was asking what it was like on the Peninsula. I asked him what sort of a time they had in Egypt. Continuing the conversation he said it had been spoiled by an excess of drill and discipline, mostly in the hands of the Adjutant who was a regular serving Officer with a seeming dislike of the Territorials. Consequently, he made himself highly unpopular by handing out punishments of one kind and another. The Adjutant was so disliked that the men had said he would be the first to by killed 'up the line'.

They moved up and took over a section of the line facing Krithia. Next day, I was in our Signal Office when casualty reports were coming in. One of those killed was the Adjutant. I wondered who had done it.

Every time I was on night duty at the Signal Office, I would be called out to go to the dugout of the General in command of one of the Brigades. His Field Telephone, quite a good instrument, was always out of order. So off I went trailing the line to see that it was still unbroken. This led straight to his dugout and, invariably, the telephone was lying on the ground outside with the lead disconnected. Carefully, I picked it up. It looked to be all right, just some polish knocked off. So I connected it to my line and called the exchange. The operator agreed it was good.

What happened regularly was that the General did not know how to hold it to hear a conversation and instead of trying, he just hurled it out of the dugout, with some bad language. What he ought to have realised was that no one would ring a Brigadier General in the night unless the situation was serious. Perhaps he was too big-headed to learn. Whatever it was, he was stupid not to learn, it put us all in danger.

Developments in Military Technology

At the same time as the fighting was taking place on Gallipoli, on the Western Front (in France and Belgium) the fighting had also reached stalemate with each side's attacks being repelled by the other. Every country's army then began to research and to use new methods of warfare. As a result there were considerable developments in military technology throughout the war.

Aeroplanes

At the start of the war, planes were seen by the Generals as toys with little use in combat, despite the fact that they had been used by Italy in 1911 in North Africa when they were at war with Ottoman Empire. In this conflict grenades and bombs had been dropped from the planes. In 1914 aircraft were very crude and were mainly used for reconnaissance, taking photographs of enemy dispositions and mapping the terrain. The pilot flew the plane whilst a photographer sitting behind leant out to take the photographs. Over time, as the war progressed, planes took over from air balloons.

Planes could only be used on relatively clear days when the pilot could see the ground to navigate, and there were no parachutes. However as the war progressed their design became more sophisticated and their speed and manoeuvrability increased.

Aeroplanes began to be used for bombing and as part of the attack when troops advanced from the trenches. Figures show that at the start of the war France had around 140 aircraft but by the end this number had increased to 4,500. They had produced 68,000 but over three quarters were lost in battle.

For planes to be of use during a battle, there needed to be a way of communicating with the ground. Wireless technology was too bulky for the planes to carry both a transmitter and a receiver, so they started flying with just the transmitter. In this way the second crew in the plane could signal to the artillery to direct their fire. This type of signalling developed so that the observer could communicate the distance from the target and the direction needed.

Before and during the Gallipoli landings the only aeroplanes available were seaplanes. These had a very low flying height and could not reach the altitudes needed to help direct the shelling from the ships. Later more planes arrived and were able to offer reconnaissance, particularly of the positions of the Turkish troops.

In January 1915 the Germans flew Zeppelins over England to bomb Great Yarmouth and Kings Lynn and the first ever aerial bombings of London took place on 31st May 1915 when 28 people were killed.

Armoured Cars and Tanks

The first armoured cars were built in the early 1900's by adding armour plating to existing motor vehicles and machine guns. The Rolls Royce Armoured Car was developed by the 2nd Duke of Westminster who took a squadron of the cars to France and fought in the Second Battle of Ypres in May 1915. After this he went to the Middle East, taking his squadron of cars, and they took part in battles in the Western Desert and in Palestine, described later in the book.

Tanks began to be developed in Britain, and the first tank came off the production line in September 1915. The track was not sufficiently robust and fell off in tests but the failures in Gallipoli pushed the emphasis of the war back to the Western Front and the politicians and the military realised there was a need for a new weapon to break the deadlock. The government officials observing the tests were impressed and further developments on the first model of the tank were ordered. By February 1916, 100 tanks, known as 'Big Willies', had been ordered by the Ministry of Munitions. In September 1916 the first mass tank attack took place on the Somme.

Poison Gas

The idea of using gas in bombs was first tried by the French and then by the Germans. Early attempts used tear gas and an irritant that made people sneeze. Developments in Germany led to the use of chlorine as a poison gas. They used it at the second battle of Ypres on 22nd April 1915. Within seconds of its use, French and Algerian troops were choking, their lungs destroyed by the gas. Panic stricken, others fled. The Germans advanced hesitantly, no doubt fearful of the effects themselves, but the Allies managed to re-form a continuous line.

There was widespread condemnation of the gas attack, which damaged German relations particularly with the USA. However in

September 1915 the British used gas too, on the Western Front. In this attack the wind conditions turned and there were more British casualties than German. Nevertheless the use of gas escalated and each soldier was issued with protection. By 1918 gas masks were issued to all frontline troops with charcoal or antidote chemical protectors. A ban on chemical weapons was eventually introduced after the war in 1925.

There is little evidence in the history books of gas ever being used on Gallipoli but the fear was that it might be and some gas protection was issued.

The Thrill and the Horror

In the trenches, the signal wires ran at the foot of the firing step and were pegged down round the traverses. We did not like them to be in the trenches because there was so much interference from digging parties, tunnelling under the Turkish trenches to blow them up. But communications were necessary and in the places where trenches were close together we had no alternative – in some cases, the enemy trench was only about 20 feet away and we could hear the Turks talking. Some of our lads used to call to them and they even exchanged food, throwing things to each other, although I doubt the Turks enjoyed our tins of bully beef when they came flying over.

The position near Gully Beach was not a friendly place; it was a hot spot and sudden death if you took a look at the countryside except by a periscope. Daylight raids were frequent to take a few prisoners, especially as the enemy knew when units were changed and they wanted to know the new occupants and to keep up their morale.

On one of those days, my comrade Jones and I were busy with a line that was intended to cross from our trench and past the left flank of the Turkish lines, down the cliff to a Naval post to be established in the valley below on the seashore. How it could be maintained I never knew, and the bright folk who thought the idea didn't either.

However, we volunteered, in a manner of speaking, to lay it, which meant us dashing out of our trench carrying a harness pack with a small drum of wire (D1) on our backs. The unfortunate part of these packs occurred when the wire did not run out continuously. You would be running along when suddenly the wire caught and you would be jerked backwards, falling on the drum of wire, which was most painful. To ease the strain, therefore, a second man ran with the carrier and pulled the wire out as they went.

The preparations were completed. We waited until it was dark and as soon as the enemy searchlight turned away from us, we climbed out of the trench and started to stumble our way to the enemy line as quietly as we could. Things were quiet. Then a bomb went off to our right. The machine gunner who played the rat-a-tat of tune was busy in the distance, and an occasional rifle shot rang out to be replied to by the enemy.

We reached the Turkish line and heard a voice speaking softly. My hair stood up and I wondered if Jones felt the same, but we kept going. He was a brave boy, Jones, he never showed fear, a true comrade. My pack made a slight squeak, it sounded like a whistle, and I prayed that the Turks couldn't hear it. A 'Verey light[15]' went up to our right and we fell flat while it burned. Then, on we went, and into the trench. Fortunately there was no one in it. We climbed out, up the other side, which was not as high as the one we came down, and we fairly rolled down the cliff-side to the shore. There we found a safe place and removed our gear. There was no sign of anyone there to receive us. Were we in the right place? We had been told to expect to see a dim

---

[15]   A flare fired into the air by a pistol often giving a greenish light.

light but after waiting for a time we decided to leave. We left the line we had laid so it could be found if anyone arrived and started to climb back, this was a much more difficult task.

When nearing the top we were spotted or heard and challenged. But at first nothing happened as we were on the Turkish side of the line so they must have thought we were their men. We fell into the trench and out, and ran as fast as we could, adrenaline and fear spurred us on. They opened fire and I thought this was it, but suddenly the firing stopped. They must have thought we might be one of their parties. We fell into our trench, breathless and sat there exhausted for some time.

Subsequently, we were told that the Navy could not get a small boat to the shore where we had left the wire, without being seen or heard at night so they abandoned the project but they forgot to tell us. Wonderful collaboration. The idea was mad anyway.

There was a lot of waiting during our time on Gallipoli, waiting for the next job, waiting for the next attack, waiting to go up the line, waiting for a message to come in or be sent. One of our principal occupations was playing games of draughts. Many of our telegraphists did night duty in Post Offices at home, and on quiet nights played draughts, so they were very skilled. Another advantage to us was the ease with which we could produce a draught board and the draughts. Our signal flags were held on wooden poles and we merely sawed off the required numbers and dipped half of them in ink. A biscuit box base with squares on it, propped on another was the board and table.

It was safer playing these games in the dugout than in the open at any time, so when we were ready to begin our game we would post a commentator to sit on the dugout steps giving us information where the shells were falling. Many of us became very expert in these games. We didn't bet on a result, because our pay was so minute we had nothing to gamble with. If we moved, we could always dump our table and board because biscuits were an issue item, and we always had a box to convert and some poles to cut into draughts.

The other games we played were cards. Some played bridge or cribbage. A crib board could be made easily by puncturing holes in a biscuit tin and using a few matches or twigs from the ground. Cribbage at one time was very popular. These opportunities occurred between our attacks when we just endured enemy shelling, persistent and dangerous at all times but this took our minds off things.

Woodcock's Medal!

My duty commenced on this particular day at 6am in the Signal Office on Hunter-Weston Hill. My unit ran the Signal Office for the 29th Division and another section was with the Naval Division.

Amongst the lines we were responsible for was one to French Headquarters in the Sedd-el-Bahr Fort. At about 9am, a terrific bombardment began from Achi Baba, the hill in front and also from the Asiatic shore across the Hellespont on our left and behind Troy, which we knew as Dardanus. The noise was tremendous and the ground shook beneath our feet. The big guns on the Asiatic side were known as 'Asiatic Annie' and another as 'Moaning Minnie'. Moaning Minnie could be heard as a thump, like a gun firing, then a long howl that gradually increased to a great crash, and then there would be a huge cloud of black smoke as it burst. These guns were all German, and ranged from 5:9's to 11-inch and 12-inch. When they each fired salvos it was quite something.

That day most of the shells were falling in the French sector, on the right of our line nearest the Asiatic shore. It wasn't long before I was called out to see to the line, which had been damaged in one of the blasts. I set off after testing it in the dugout, running straight into the smoke of the bombardment, and fortunately I soon came upon the break. The wire was our D5 cable with a copper core and steel strands round it, then a covering of rubber and waterproofed cotton. It was in fact a good strong wire. A repair meant joining the copper strands and enclosing it with a rubber sleeve about 4 inches long. It wasn't an easy task when under such heavy fire but it focussed your mind away from the shelling.

That day, as the bombardment continued, I had to walk backwards and forwards along the trenches as the shells continued to burst and damage the line. To miss the shells I occasionally dropped into a dugout then out again testing the line. I went off towards French HQ because our Generals needed communication with them to provide support. The French troops were all in the dugouts as this was a particularly heavy attack. Even the gunners had left their guns and come in to shelter from the bombardment. There were many casualties among them, some quite revolting, where a shell had burst near and disembowelled them. These were big shells and they made such a mess of men in dugouts.

That day, I repaired the line in 52 places and kept it working but by 4pm, after ten hours working on my own under fire and not having had any rest, food or water, I was exhausted. However, it was a cardinal rule that a linesman remained on his line to keep it open until he was called in, but I felt compelled to ask the NCO in charge of the Signal Office to send a relief as the line was then working. He was annoyed and reluctantly agreed to Baxter relieving me. Baxter arrived at 4.30pm. I struggled back to our lines and, shattered, I fell into my dugout.

The bombardment ceased at 5pm and Baxter returned. He was subsequently awarded the Serbian Gold Cross, which became known in our unit as 'Woodcock's Medal'. What mystified me was why he was decorated with the Serbian Gold Cross. We had no Serbs with the Campaign. Indeed few could say where Serbia was!

I never knew how decorations for bravery in the Army were allocated during a war. I saw many instances that went unnoticed, and many medals awarded for nothing – I was to learn. Soon after the original Gallipoli landings, I was on duty when a message came through the Signal Office from General Ian Hamilton, Commander-in-Chief, addressed to the Divisional Generals to the effect that there were so many Military Crosses, D.S.O.'s[16], D.C.M.'s[17], Military Medals and Foreign Decorations

---

[16] The Distinguished Service Order (D.S.O.) was awarded for an act of distinguished service when under fire or in the presence of the enemy. Between 1914 and 1916 it was awarded to some staff officers when they were not in contact with the enemy. This was not well received and it was restricted again to those under fire, in 1917.

[17] Distinguished Service Order (D.S.O.) and The Distinguished Conduct Medal (D.C.OM.) was the medal awarded to recognise an act of gallantry in the field by a member of the armed forces who was below the rank of officer.

to be awarded. They had decided the number in advance! The communication gave Division and Brigade Commanders orders to submit recommendations. Like the rations, they had 'come up' for distribution. In due course, lists came through and these were sent to General HQ to be vetted. Later they were awarded. This was a regular procedure all during the Campaign. Many brave deeds went unrecognised.

The Suvla Landings, August, 1915

Within a few days of the landings in April a stalemate was reached that remained despite the many battles. Lines were drawn across the south of the Peninsula around Cape Helles and in a semicircle around Anzac Cove. In London the stalemate on Gallipoli had repercussions. The divisions that existed before over whether the Army should have been sent to France instead still persisted. Churchill described the atmosphere in one War Council meeting as 'sulphurous'.

After the failure of the navy to force the Dardanelles, the relationship in the Admiralty between Churchill and Fisher began to deteriorate. Fisher wanted to withdraw ships from the seas around Gallipoli to prevent torpedo attacks, whilst Churchill wanted to send more ships accompanied by submarines. Churchill in his political position heading the Admiralty also persisted in sending orders to the admirals in the Mediterranean despite Fisher, as overall commander of the navy, telling him not to interfere. Their arguing culminated in Fisher's resignation in mid-May. At the same time the government was in trouble partly due to the problems in both France and Gallipoli but mostly due to the shortage of munitions for all the fighting forces.

The Churchill-Fisher clash brought things to a head and on 17th May 1915 the Prime Minister, Herbert Asquith, told the King that a coalition government was needed. In the negotiations that followed to form the coalition, the Conservative Party made sure that Churchill (then in the Liberal Party) was removed from the Admiralty. He was given a Cabinet position with no authority as Chancellor of the Duchy of Lancaster but this did not stop his interest in Gallipoli.

How to break the stalemate on Gallipoli became the burning question. Opinions, once again were split. Churchill circulated a paper supporting fresh landings north of Anzac near Bulair. Others thought this was too hazardous. The Cabinet decided they needed first-hand information from Gallipoli. Asquith decided to send Churchill together with the Cabinet Secretary Maurice Hankey to report on matters but Churchill withdrew from the visit under pressure from his colleagues. Rumours of his visit circulated on Gallipoli. Hankey had real misgivings about going but set off nevertheless.

In June the decision was finally taken to try another offensive on Gallipoli to break the deadlock. General Hamilton was informed that reinforcements were on their way. They were to be from Kitchener's 'New Army', Territorial Army divisions plus new recruits, men with little training or experience of fighting. Hamilton was told that there would be plenty of ammunition too. Plans were drawn up for an attack across the north of the Peninsula from Anzac Cove to Kilia Bay on the Dardanelles, supported by a landing of new troops just north at Suvla Bay.

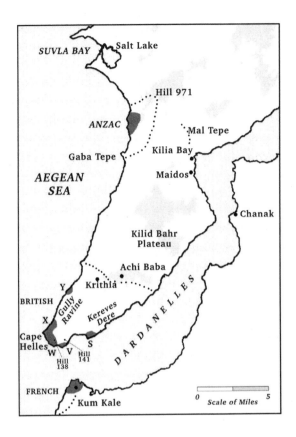

The Gallipoli Peninsula showing Suvla Bay, Anzac Cove and Kilia Bay

Who was to command the new forces and direct the offensive? Hamilton asked Kitchener for someone experienced, and put forward the names of two officers who he knew had commanded in France with distinction. Military hierarchy and poor leadership intervened. The commander of one of the divisions involved in the Suvla offensive said that he would refuse to accept orders from either of Hamilton's nominees since both were junior in rank to him. Rather than tackle this issue, Hamilton allowed Kitchener to appoint the only person available with a higher rank, General Sir Frederick Stopford.

Frederick Stopford had retired from the army six years earlier due to ill health and had no combat experience at all but he was appointed. As a result, the most important offensive to break the deadlock in the war was to be led by an inexperienced general, commanding inexperienced troops.

Hamilton took on board the lessons from the landings in April. Water was to be pumped ashore. Hospitals, ammunition dumps and food supplies were all planned. A ship was to lay a cable from Hamilton's headquarters on Imbros to the bay so he would be in touch with Stopford. Troops were to be landed under the cover of darkness in newly acquired landing vessels called 'beetles'. There was great secrecy with no reconnaissance of the area and no flying over the bay. Everything was kept secret to the point that the maps were not issued until it was almost too late for the officers to familiarise themselves with the lie of the land. As there were no flights over the area, there was no information about Turkish troop dispositions either.

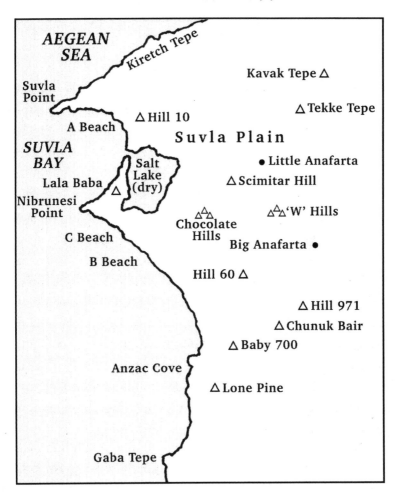

Suvla Bay showing the landing beaches and the key areas of the battle

Hamilton went through the plans with Stopford on 22nd July. Broadly, the troops landing in Suvla Bay were to set off quickly, with the benefit of surprise, to capture the high ground around the bay and hold it, whilst the bulk of the troops went south to support the main offensive from Anzac Cove. Here the Anzac forces were to break out of their lines, capturing Lone Pine, Baby 700 and Chunuk Bair (see map of Suvla Bay). With support from the large force of troops landed at Suvla Bay, they would then push on across the Peninsula to Kilia Bay.

Stopford went through the plans with his chief of staff, who raised some objections. Together they made changes described now by military historians as 'substantial modifications'. Surprisingly Hamilton did not intervene. As a result the orders that were eventually issued for the landings included words like 'if possible' and had no deadlines for capturing some of the key hilltop areas. More importantly though, the revised plans did not mention that landings were taking place to support the main push from Anzac towards Kilia Bay, and as a result one of the leading commanders thought that the Anzac offensive was actually taking place to distract the Turks from the landings at Suvla Bay!

Troops began to land under the cover of darkness, hiding on shore each night from the 4th August with the main landings taking place during the night of the 6th and into the day of the 7th August. They achieved complete surprise, and the Anzac offensive then began as planned. However things soon began to go awry. Military historians agree that General Stopford completely failed to exploit the opportunity that lay within his reach and confusion reigned.

Some of the forces, lacking good maps, went inland and became lost. Others were rested on the beach by their senior officers until the artillery came ashore. Most importantly, there was little or no help given to the Anzac forces to support their operation to cross the Peninsula towards Kilia Bay.

Hamilton had one of his men on shore, Lieutenant Colonel Aspinall-Oglander, who was with the Cabinet Secretary, Maurice Hankey. Both were dismayed at what they found. On the beach they found lethargy, with no one seeming to realise the need to press into action at speed and with the benefit of surprise. Aspinall tried to do something about it but the commander he spoke to (the one who thought the Anzac offensive was there as a distraction) said his troops were exhausted and anyway he had no orders to move forward, at least that was how he interpreted his orders.

Not being able to report back in confidence using Stopford's line of communication, Aspinall got on a boat and went out to send a message via the naval lines from the flagship. On board he found a furious naval commander, Roger Keyes who had already cabled Hamilton urging him to come to Suvla. Aspinall sent a similar message saying that golden opportunities were being lost and the situation was very serious. Communications being what they were, Hamilton did not receive Keyes' message at all and Aspinall's arrived the next morning. The Cabinet Secretary, Hankey later wrote to the prime minister saying that a peaceful scene had greeted them on their arrival on shore, exactly the opposite of what he had expected.

The next day Hamilton tried to get himself to Suvla Bay. Incredibly, he was told that no ship was available. He had to wait until one became available that evening. As a result he did not come ashore until it was too late. By then General Liman-Von-Sanders, Hamilton's German opposite commanding the Turkish forces, had acted. Unlike Hamilton, once he realised what was happening with the landings he immediately reorganised his forces. He removed the commanders he thought were not up to the battle and gave command of all the troops in the region of Suvla Bay to someone he knew could lead – Mustafa Kemal Atatürk.

Despite having been awake for two nights with the fighting at Anzac, when he got the call Mustafa Kemal got on his horse and rode across the hills in the darkness to take charge of the action to repel the British invasion. Not surprisingly, it is said that he took something to keep himself awake. His reinforcements arrived during the night and, after reviewing the situation, Kemal decided to attack along the whole line. This meant sending his troops up to the hilltops – the ones the British should have taken immediately after landing – then charging down the other side onto the Suvla plains. The British were just on their way up the slopes, all too late, when the Turks charged over the top, annihilating them. The dry bushes on the plain caught fire; retreating British soldiers were burned.

Hamilton watched the chaos from his ship offshore. After two hours, the Turkish attack died down and Hamilton went ashore to find Stopford supervising the building of a hut for his headquarters.

Kemal now turned his attention to the battle at Anzac. Again he reviewed the situation with his officers and ordered an attack along the whole line. His men were exhausted from the battle and to encourage them he told them that he would go first. He crawled out into no man's land, stood up and walked towards the British lines. Only his watch was damaged in the attack. His men followed. By the end of the fighting the Turks had regained all their trenches; none of the key hills were in British hands. The landings had failed.

Mustafa Kemal Atatürk's victory here and in later battles made him a hero. He went on to lead the Turkish war of independence and to become the President of Turkey until his death in 1938. On the British side heads began to roll. First Stopford was removed. When his replacement arrived, the commander who had previously refused to serve under anyone junior to him, demanded to be relieved of his command and he went too. Many others followed.

Once back in London Stopford added to the feeling of mistrust of Hamilton, particularly in defence of himself. The arrival of a journalist, Keith Murdoch, sealed Hamilton's fate.

During the war the press were censored and restricted, however, two correspondents, Ellis Ashmead-Bartlett, who wrote for the London papers, and Lester Lawrence of Reuters, who wrote for the provincial papers, were attached to the Dardanelles expedition. Bartlett was very critical of Hamilton and the leadership of the campaign throughout. He often predicted disaster, and much to the annoyance of the Generals he was often right. He predicted the sinking of the *Majestic*, the boat on which he was accommodated the day before it was torpedoed – he was rescued. But it was the censors that drew his frustration. Then Keith Murdoch arrived.

On his way to London to take up a post in Fleet Street, the Australian journalist, Keith Murdoch, – father of Rupert – stopped off and was given permission by Hamilton to visit Anzac Cove. He signed the war correspondents' declaration saying he would submit what he wrote to the censor at headquarters and headed off. Despite military personnel being forbidden from speaking to the press, there were plenty of Australian and New Zealand troops who were more than prepared to tell him of the horrors and he was said to have been genuinely appalled by what he heard.

Murdoch returned to Imbros and met up with Bartlett who realised that this was a perfect opportunity for him to get his story of military incompetence back to the authorities in London – avoiding the censors. He gave Murdoch his story to take with him to London and crossed his fingers. In it he said that, in his opinion, a major catastrophe was about to happen unless something was done.

Unfortunately, on his way to London Keith Murdoch was searched by military police in Marseilles and Bartlett's story was confiscated. There had been a spy in the camp listening to the discussion between the journalists who alerted the authorities. However, as soon as Murdoch arrived in England he prepared his own, much more vivid account, which rapidly circulated around Whitehall. Even the Prime Minister, Asquith, circulated Murdoch's report and it was put before the War Council as well as the Dardanelles Committee before General Hamilton or any of his staff had had chance to see it or comment.

In his diary, Maurice Hankey, secretary to the War Council, wrote on the 24th September 1915: 'I lunched with Mr Balfour to meet a horrible scab called Murdoch, an Australian journalist, who had written a poisonous letter to Fisher[18], the Commonwealth Premier, re. the Dardanelles'.

This sealed Hamilton's fate. On October 15th he was recalled and replaced with Sir Charles Monro, someone who was firmly on the side of the war being fought in France.

---

[18] Andrew Fisher was the Australian Prime Minister

A Break (of Sorts) From the Fighting

In July 1915, while the Gallipoli Campaign was in full flood, some of my section were ordered to the island of Imbros 'for a rest', or so it was said. We were delighted to be leaving for a break from the shelling.

We went from W beach by way of a converted trawler. A fierce battle was in progress, and as we sailed round the tip of the Peninsula we passed a flat bottomed gun boat, called a monitor, with a huge gun on it, about 15 inches. It fired as we were passing and we looked to see where the shell burst. It hit the cliff with a tremendous crash, for the sailors had failed to elevate the gun before firing. On the cliff top was a marquee where a parson was holding a service for the boys who were going into action, and that rocked about as if in a gale of wind. We watched and laughed as all the soldiers scrambled out to take cover.

We certainly did look forward to a rest, having been under constant fire without respite since the landings in April, and we set out cheerfully in the trawler. We had a good crossing; the sea was calm and the sun shone. As we got further away from the Peninsula, you could almost imagine you were on holiday with the blue sky, turquoise sea and gently lapping waves.

We arrived at our landing place. A small pier had been made by placing bags of cement on the sea bottom and building up the pier from this base. General Hamilton's Headquarters were on the island. He was there with his staff, covered in all the red tabs with coloured caps and armbands. Everyone had highly polished boots too and short canes, all the badges of rank.

Upon arrival, we reported to GHQ. To our astonishment, we were told to take over a Pack Wireless Station up on the cliff-top and arrange 24-hour shifts. To this we complained that we had only been sent for a rest, but the reply was: 'Yes, from the shelling, but not from work'. There was neither leave nor time off in those days. Neither was there a canteen for a beer, it didn't matter though because we hadn't had any pay, so we had to make the best of it. We belonged to GHQ Signal Company but always seemed to find ourselves helping other units in difficulty.

When we went on duty, we took our blankets to take advantage of quiet periods, but we need not have worried, for like everything else there, the wireless didn't work!

The wireless station had a 20-foot mast, an aerial suspended on two poles, two wires about twenty feet long, with an earth mat of woven copper, rather like a golden stair carpet, 24 inches wide, a beautiful thing really. The generator was run by a Douglas motorcycle engine. The station could receive messages in Morse code from about 100 miles away and it could send out messages for 30 miles. The tuner was like those subsequently used in crystal wireless sets made when the war ended.

We made some repairs but the signals we heard on the earphones varied from very high pitched to very low grunts, and it was necessary to constantly tune to find out what station was required. One man listened while the others slept or until the generator was required. We had, in our training in England, to use signal codes and send and receive messages in Morse. There was a codebook supplied with this kit. It had a cover made of lead, which was inscribed, 'If this book is in danger of being captured by an enemy it must be thrown overboard'. 'It will sink' was underlined. Inside was a three letter code. 'EXF', for example, translated as 'Enemy ship sighted on port bow', as this was a Naval codebook. It wasn't any use to us on land.

In the harbour under the cliff battleships, cruisers, destroyers and smaller landing craft were preparing for the landings on Suvla. We listened in. The Fleet, or part of it, were in the harbour below to escape attention from a submarine. Messages were being sent from ship to ship and to shore, mostly about washing or invitations to lunch and dinners (Officers only). The idea of going out to dinner was like being in outer space to us! We had been on Gallipoli with little water and poor food and here were the Officers dining well on a quiet Greek island.

Listening in to the messages was always on the fine tunings, or so it seemed, and when the battleship *Triad* began its loud deep bass, very strong signal, it precluded us from hearing anything else and so we retired to rest again. Incidentally, quite a lot of her messages seemed to be about the ship's laundry!

Altogether, it was a very pleasant break but our return was rough in the trawlers. We were seasick and glad to be back on dry land, although not to dodge the shells on Gallipoli again!

The Pack Wireless Station on Imbros really was useless. We never received any messages to pass on to any of the GHQ staff. Neither did we know what happened to it in the evacuation. It would probably have been a casualty and broken up.

The landings at Suvla took place a few days afterwards in August when all the Fleet and landing craft departed. There were great expectations that this action would outflank the others at Helles and Anzac. We waited to hear news with anticipation, hoping that it would bring the victory we all wanted, but it didn't. It was a badly organised affair.

From the messages we received it looked like another bungled effort by Stopford, a retired Boer War General brought back. We heard that he calmly started to set up Headquarters by the seacoast and lost touch with his Battalions, some marched inland and were never heard of again, others went in the wrong direction. It was a complete muddle. Hamilton at GHQ could not find out what was happening. We picked up some messages but none of value to a Commander so he went to Suvla to roust them. That was it. The Turks hurriedly moved forces down and ours were held. It signified the end of Gallipoli. That was in August. Our leaders had thrown away the lives of several Divisions of troops through bad planning and bad organisation.

Lessons in Leadership from our Officers and Generals

Gallipoli had Generals brought back from retirement yet expected to fight an Army modernised to some extent but not altogether. Men whose sole idea was to appear on a parade with everything cleaned by a Batman and say, 'Carry on Sergeant Major' and leave him to run the unit. The Germans were no better in that respect than we were. Our Commander in Chief, Hamilton, was a 62-year-old poet, non-smoker, teetotaller, out of touch and could not organise. I was with him in battle when he used a telescope to observe the enemy whom I could see easily with the naked eye. No matter what our losses were, he was always cheerful.

Hamilton's arrangements for the Suvla landings were typical. When things went wrong he wasn't there to put them right – and couldn't get there either. Stopford was the General in Charge and another useless one. He was also 62. Hamilton didn't know the dispositions; he left that with Braithwaite, his so-called Planner, and, of course, the Generals on the spot. They sat on the beach for a time, no opposition, then marched inland. Whole Battalions were never seen again. Like us at Helles, they had no transport ashore, no supplies, no ammunition. They hadn't learned from the landings in April!

Before the war, the Regular Army Officers were recruited mainly from a few select boarding schools. The young men were the sons of Army Officers or friends, and it was virtually impossible to rise from the ranks to a Commission. They went from school directly to a unit. Technical training was negligible. Officers were trained in the use of arms – a rifle and some a machine gun. The Cavalry, the pride of the Army, were taught to ride horses, and drill. In 1914 they were still being trained to fight in the style of the wars of the last century, ridiculous!

Our Lieutenant was Acting General on the Southern Signal company manoeuvres in 1914 to examine their efficiency. He was by occupation a bank clerk. He was also one of the best horse riders we ever had. He was very efficient; always a gentleman. We never had another with his capabilities. The men would do anything he asked and we, of course, trained with

147

him. He was badly wounded by a shell burst in June 1915 and his life was saved by our men carrying him to hospital and, fortunately, he was put straight on board a ship and back to England. He recovered well enough from his wounds and went to France with the Tank Corps Signals, and was promoted to Colonel. His name was Jackson.

An Officer's life on Gallipoli was reckoned to be in the region of 24 hours. At the start they went into action in spanking uniforms with Sam Browne belts, a revolver in one hand, a sword in the other, at the head of their platoon. Needless to say, they were killed first. The average Officer realised the need for change but it was slow in coming. Some units were without an Officer for longish periods. Our unit was without after our first was badly wounded, so we had only a Sergeant in command for some time. The replacements that arrived were untrained, inexperienced in command and generally useless. Soon they were also killed, wounded or taken sick.

After Jackson we had a succession of duds, with gaps between when we had no one. Indeed, it seemed we could not keep Officers. None of them who came in 1915 or afterwards knew anything about our signals work apart from reading a manual issued pre-war. The work changed entirely in wartime and the NCO's were the leaders and experts. The Officer replacements, instead of being from our ranks, were from the Infantry chiefly. Fellows who knew how to use the flags, something we never used, or used very little. Most of them could not ride. They had to be taught, since ours was a mounted unit. One fellow from the 4th Royal Scots came in plaid trousers. He knew what a horse looked like but that was all. Feeding, grooming, exercising, yes he thought he could learn! He used to ride his horse in a kilt, which can't have been comfortable.

Another Officer arrived, he was short-sighted but refused to admit it. He fell over everything, and if there was any wire about he became entangled in it. Fair play to him, he insisted on seeing all the lines we had but because of his eyesight he wanted to see them in daylight. Considering that many had to be run out at night because of being under fire it was most risky, and we told him so, but we took him anyway – orders were orders!

On one occasion I had to run out an attack line and he insisted on coming with me. We had quite an easy task on the first day, and he really thought there was nothing dangerous in it except an odd shell or two but as we got nearer the line and into the support trenches things heated up. When we got back I said that from then on it would be night work, and he agreed.

What a time he had, tripping over barbed wire, falling into dugouts and trenches. He was as blind as a bat at night but quite undaunted until a 'Verey light', went up just in front of him. I dropped down but I saw him standing in the bright light as shots rang out. He fell and it took about 5 minutes to find him. We walked along the trench but couldn't find a way out. Poor fellow, he was shaken but insisted on going on to complete the job. I noticed that when he carried the telephone in its base he put it on his shoulder nearest the enemy lines, to protect his head presumably. We stumbled back to our lines before daylight. He never asked to go out again at night, and two weeks later he went to hospital with dysentery. We did not see him again. The Peninsula took its toll.

Sometimes the incompetence of our Officers caused friction. Once, when I was a Sergeant Major, the Officer and I visited a working party. He said they were not doing the work in accordance with the training manual. I replied that it had been out of date from 1914. He got so hot under the collar that he said he would have me Court Martialled. I asked him what he knew about that as well! Nothing came of it.

The Decision to Evacuate

Before setting off to replace General Hamilton, Sir Charles Monro studied the files in the War Office and spoke to key people. On arrival in the region, he visited each of the landing sites at Suvla, Anzac and Cape Helles and spoke to the divisional generals. There had been storms on Gallipoli and the weather had turned cold. No winter clothing had arrived, and supplies were so low that the British guns were restricted to two shells per day. He found very low morale amongst the troops and very poor living conditions. The following day he sent a message to Kitchener recommending the evacuation.

Hamilton had estimated that up to half the troops would die if the Peninsula was evacuated. Monro's estimate was around 40,000 men. In London there was concern about Britain's reputation in the world, particularly the Muslim world, if the evacuation took place. There was also concern about the fate of Egypt and the possibility of Russia signing a peace deal with the Germans. It was recognised, however, that a voluntary withdrawal, carefully planned, would mean fewer troops would die than if the Turks launched an offensive that pushed the Allied forces into the sea.

The wrangling between the politicians and the military leaders about what to do went on for several months. In the meantime, Bulgaria declared on the side of Germany and began to mobilise so an Allied force was sent to Salonika (now Thessaloniki) to provide support to Serbia. Two divisions were sent from Gallipoli.

With no decision forthcoming, the navy began to think again about forcing the Dardanelles with the remaining minesweepers and battleships in the Mediterranean. Lord Kitchener was against an evacuation and liked the idea put forward by the navy. He began working on the plans with Admiral Keyes, who was back in London for a short time before returning to the Mediterranean fleet.

Once the plans for another attempt to force the Dardanelles were developed, Kitchener sent a secret message to Birdwood, 'his man' on Gallipoli, who was commanding the Anzac forces, telling him to make plans to gather as many of the troops of fighting strength together for a new landing at the Gulf of Xeros. Realising that Monro would oppose this, Kitchener decided that he would be moved to lead the forces in Salonika and that Birdwood would lead the new landings. When he was informed of this, Birdwood suppressed the message and told Kitchener he wanted Monro to remain in charge. He did not believe that the plans had any hope of success, and he certainly did not want to be in charge!

Kitchener then left London for Gallipoli, stopping off in Paris on the way. There the French told him they were also against an evacuation and would be willing to support a naval attack on the Dardanelles. Kitchener sent a message to Keyes to join him in Marseilles so they could draw up the detailed plans together as they sailed to Gallipoli. Once again poor communication intervened. Keyes never got the message. The officer on duty in the Admiralty did not pass the message on, thinking Keyes did not have time to get to Marseilles before the boat sailed (he did). When Keyes did not turn up in Marseilles, Kitchener concluded that the naval attack was off. Meanwhile in fact, Keyes was in Paris and had gained agreement for at least six warships to join the attack.

When he arrived in the region in early November, Kitchener had to mediate between the Egyptian high commissioner who did not want the evacuation to go ahead, Monro who did and the naval commanders who favoured another attack on the Dardanelles.

After visiting the troops on the Peninsula, Kitchener acknowledged that the terrain was much more difficult than he had imagined and that the Turks were well dug in with fortress-like defences. After visiting Anzac and Suvla Bay he cabled the War Office saying he had decided to evacuate this territory and consolidate at Cape Helles.

At the end of November, just after Kitchener left, there was a violent storm on the Peninsula with hurricane force winds followed by several days of sleet and snow and severe frosts. In some areas men on both sides, Turks and British, had to climb out of their trenches to avoid being drowned. No boats could land for several days and supplies dwindled. Without winter equipment the men began to suffer. Records show that British forces were reduced by a tenth, and morale could not have got any lower.

Complex as it was, several factors combined to make the final decision to evacuate. The men on Gallipoli were clearly not fighting fit and were not up to a renewed landing. There was a fear that if the navy failed to force the Dardanelles then there would be no ships left to help with an evacuation should one be necessary.

By the end of August 1915 the Central Powers had occupied Poland and the Russians were almost eliminated as a threat to them on the Eastern Front. As a result the Germans and Austro-Hungarians regrouped and refocused their efforts on the Western

Front. This created pressure for Allied troops to be redeployed to France.

With the loss of Poland, the Russian economy went into turmoil and as thousands of refugees flooded into Russia together with the retreating soldiers, civil unrest began. This was to have an effect later in the war. By the end of 1915, the Tsar had taken over as head of the Russian army in order to continue the war on the Eastern Front, but Russia was now a much reduced force and much less of a threat to the Germans.

Finally, the French and Russians intervened in the decision making about a new landing elsewhere on the Peninsula. Bulgaria had just joined the war on the side of Germany and the Central Powers and had begun to move into Serbia. France and Russia said they would not allow troops to be taken from the front in Salonika, where they were supporting Serbia, to help with a new landing.

On the 7th December 1915, the decision was finally made to evacuate the Peninsula.

The End of the Line on Gallipoli

No one in England seemed interested after the original landings were a failure. The letters from home told us that our war on Gallipoli wasn't being reported.

In September it rained heavily and we were flooded. It was about this time that evacuation was first mentioned. The big August battles were costly in lives and were failures. Nevertheless, we were ordered to start digging winter quarters for ourselves and our horses 12 feet deep. No covering was ever supplied, so we draped bell tents over them, which was not very good.

Everybody by now was fed up. We were gradually realising the hopelessness of our task. It was a brainchild of Churchill, and he was in disfavour. He had no idea of the magnitude of the job. We were slowly being eliminated. There was always a shortage of wood. All the trees had been knocked down by shellfire, so we burnt them to help the tea making. Many of our signal poles had the same fate. They burned well but it meant we had nothing left to burn to keep ourselves warm when the temperature dropped. In October, everything froze and the trenches were slippery. Water again became scarce, and there were hundreds of cases of frostbite. The sea in the Levant was noted for being rough in winter and supplies began to run short as the boats couldn't get ashore with our supplies.

This then was the world in which we lived and died. Each day brought the realisation that things were becoming hopeless. Various attacks were unsuccessful. Turkish snipers behind our lines were a nuisance day and night. Frightened of submarines, the Fleet had gone off with all our heavy Artillery and abandoned us, at least that is how we felt. Not that they were any better than the Army but it was comforting to see them in the bay. Naval firing, as I have already said, was dreadfully inaccurate. They fired into our men on so many occasions, and their long-range shells were useless on land as the trajectory was too flat. They lost the *Majestic* and then some old battleships and were frightened of losing more, so the Fleet departed. They couldn't silence the Turkish and German guns on Achi Baba or on the Asiatic side. They had failed to stop the German ships (the *Breslau* and *Goeben*) from going up the Dardanelles at the start of the war, and these two ships were a continual menace to us all through the Campaign. So it dragged on.

We hung on until November. Word was passed to us that Churchill the promoter was coming. We all bet that he wouldn't come. Someone must have warned him his life would not be worth an hour's purchase if he had landed. He sent Kitchener instead who arrived, looked around one day and departed. After half an hour on shore at Helles (appropriately named), he ordered the evacuation. We were leaving at last.

Preparations began at Suvla Bay but the troops were not told until early December. We wondered how the Turks would react. Would they try to prevent us in our weakened state or be glad to see us go? That was the question. When Suvla was evacuated all the Turkish guns there were moved against us in the south of the Peninsula, and when Anzac was evacuated we had even more against us. Naturally, the Turks knew that we were evacuating, although we were told to make it look as if we were staying.

After the enemy guns moved to Helles we underwent daily and nightly bombardment of growing intensity. It was as if the Turks wanted to blow us off. The 29th Division had gone to Suvla in October and we were moved to the 9th Corps to work, but gradually there was little to do but take cover. Shells broke everything down. Communication trenches became shallow ditches with little cover in places. We spent time building them up. In the night, ships came and loaded then disappeared before daybreak. Troops marching down to embark turned about and marched towards the line whenever a hostile plane was over. Gadgets of all kinds were fitted up to fire every now and then to appear to the Turks that we were all still there.

Then we were ordered to make our preparations. We had orders to go down to V beach, where we had originally landed. Everything that could be was to be destroyed. We destroyed our wagons and our remaining stores. Our few remaining horses were to be left behind. We could not believe it – leave the horses – Never! But we did. I gave Timbuc all the sugar I had saved from my meagre rations and petted him – stroked him – said goodbye and then, in the dark, we made our way down the trail to the beach to board a small steamer that in peace time sailed from Holyhead to Dublin.

It was a night of mixed emotions, relief that we were leaving at last but tremendous sadness at having to leave my beloved

Timbuc. I could only hope that the Turks would recognise what a wonderful animal he was and treat him well.

We had to be off before daylight otherwise we should be shelled from the Asiatic shore and blown out of the water, as we were only about 2 miles away. After we embarked, the sea came up rough and the lighters that were alongside threatened to stave in the ship's sides. Just before daylight, as we were becoming anxious because we would be under open observation to the gunners on the Asiatic side of the Hellespont, the engines started and we moved off. Had we stayed another 20 minutes they would have blown us out of the water. No ship had been there in daylight for some weeks.

How glad we were to come away. Not long after we set sail the singing began – we sang all the way to Imbros.

Churchill's Legacy

I can never forgive Churchill for what he brought about on Gallipoli. He conceived the invasion and pushed it on the War Cabinet. The plan was flawed from the start. With the advent of the submarine, our ships could not possibly have supplied Russia. The journey through the Mediterranean and into the Dardanelles was, at that point, too hazardous even for our war ships, let alone a merchant fleet. His plans proved useless and were thrown overboard with thousands of the lives of young, eager volunteers who rose to the call of their country in its predicament. If he had landed on the Peninsula as we had been told he would, his life would have been half an hour there. Someone would have shot him. I saw things happen there that I would not have believed: the ground covered with dead bodies and the sickly sweet smell of death everywhere.

So sad. So very, very sad.

I'm sorry if I'm repeating myself but the whole Campaign was a sorry tale of bad planning and inefficient Generals and Admirals. There was plenty of enthusiasm amongst the troops, who were badly led by Officers, without anything but courage. All those good, healthy, smart, joyful boys slaughtered time after time in attacks arranged by so-called Planners who had no idea. The landings should have been elsewhere, not where defences were strongest; the wrong places were chosen.

We left so many of our comrades behind, one might say the flower of the youth of our Islands and Australia and New Zealand, who fought so tenaciously at Anzac. The total number of troops engaged was half a million. The losses in 10 months were 250,000 killed and wounded. The Turks lost as many as us. They all, except the 29th Division, were volunteers and Territorials. The Navy failed to force the narrows. We failed to take the land. It must have cost millions of pounds.

In my mind, I have always regarded this Campaign as the one that really meant the end of the British Empire. It was the writing on the wall.

The Evacuation: Getting Out At Last

At Anzac the Turkish trenches were very close, so the men at the front could not be taken off until the last minute. Various devices were made to fire rifles and set off bombs after the troops departed to make it sound as if they were still there. Booby traps and mines were laid to stop a fast advance should the Turks realise what was happening. It was not until daylight when everyone was off that the Turks became suspicious of the quiet and moved forward. The Turks then moved all their forces south to Cape Helles. There the evacuation was to be more difficult with heavy fire from the Turkish guns.

The evacuation of Cape Helles was interrupted by bad weather, and took longer than planned. On the day before the last troops were to be withdrawn, the Turks launched a fierce artillery bombardment. Every available remaining soldier was brought into the defence of the British trenches. There was plenty of ammunition, and it needed to be used up before they left. The Turks suffered severe losses; the fighting died away as night fell. The following day the sun shone and final preparations to leave were made. Everything went to plan and by the morning of the 9th January 1916 there were no British troops left on the Peninsula, save for the bodies of those who had died during the campaign.

With careful planning and good organisation the evacuation of all the forces had taken place with no loss of life.

Turkish morale soared with their victory. The Germans now had more troops available and could redeploy their armaments to other fronts. Countries not previously involved began to join the war on the side of the Germans, since they appeared the most likely victors. In Britain the press ran stories about the horrors of the campaign and about the mistakes and bungling of the politicians and the Generals. The affect on morale at home in Britain gave rise to concern at the highest level.

Winston Churchill was widely blamed for the failures of Gallipoli. His reputation was rock bottom. He made his last speech in the House of Commons in November 1915, resigned from his government post and set off to France to fight on the Western Front.

The fear at that point was that Turkish forces would be redeployed to attack Egypt and the Suez Canal. A new campaign was to begin.

PART II

GREECE, EGYPT, PALESTINE AND FRANCE

Salonika: Supporting Serbia

On leaving Gallipoli, my grandfather set sail for Salonika, now Thessaloniki, to join the British and French forces there to provide support to Serbia against the Central Powers (Turkey and the Ottoman Empire, Germany, Austria-Hungary and now Bulgaria).

Greece, Salonika and Serbia

Within a week of their declaration of war on Serbia in July 1914, the Austro-Hungarian Empire found itself at war with Russia, one of the largest armies in the world at that time. The result was that Serbia became a much smaller and almost forgotten war in the wider scheme of things. In the first year of the war, Serbian losses were tremendous, but the Serbs held out, supplied with ammunition from France and Greece.

Following the failure of the Turks to take the Suez Canal early in 1915, and with Romania allied to Russia, and Bulgaria remaining neutral, the Germans realised that taking Serbia was the key to being able to link Germany to Constantinople by train to enable them to send military supplies to the Turks. The fighting in Serbia intensified. In the meantime, the Germans began to woo the Bulgarians, trying to get them on side by promising them the land back that they had lost in the Balkan Wars.

Almost too late the Allies realised that they needed to help Serbia but getting there was not easy with Serbia landlocked. Greece held the key but there was a split between the Greek prime minister, who was pro the Allies, and the King who was pro German. When Bulgaria declared on the side of the Germans in September 1915, and began mobilising, the Greek prime minister gave permission to the French and British to land at Salonika. Soon afterwards the King of Greece sacked the prime minister and handed a military fort in Macedonia to the Germans. This split led to a civil war in Greece, which culminated in the abdication of the King and the country being reunified in 1917 under the prime minister and declaring on the side of the Allies.

When the Greek prime minister gave the French and British permission to land at Salonika, and to march from there into

Serbia, they sent two divisions – some of these being the same troops that had fought at Gallipoli.

On 7th October 1915, the Austria-Hungarian and German armies began a serious offensive to defeat Serbia. Crossing the Danube they reached the capital, Belgrade, which fell on the 9th October. A week later the Bulgarians attacked Serbia from two directions. The Serbian Army was divided. The army in central Serbia retreated to the west, where around 300,000 soldiers and civilians attempted to cross the Albanian mountains in the middle of winter – more than 100,000 died on the way. Meanwhile the soldiers in the south joined the Allies but, by December 1915, all the Allies were back in Greece at Salonika.

With Serbia defeated, the railway from Berlin to Constantinople was finally opened and able to supply the Turkish forces against the British elsewhere in the Middle East.

On 4th December 1915, Maurice Hankey, Secretary to the War Cabinet, crossed the Channel for a conference with the French to decide on the future of the war in Serbia. The decision was taken to withdraw from Salonika but within a couple of days the French changed their minds and rescinded the agreement.

On the 7th December, the Cabinet met and agreed the evacuation of Suvla Bay and Anzac on Gallipoli. No decision was taken about Salonika. Hankey became extremely frustrated saying: 'They put off decisions, squabble, have no plan of action or operation and allowed themselves to be dragged into this miserable Salonika affair at the tail of French domestic politics.' Whilst they were not withdrawing from Salonika, the British decided not to send more troops; some of the boats carrying soldiers from Gallipoli were turned around, including the one carrying my grandfather.

In March 1916 the French again persuaded the British not to leave Salonika. During the first four months of 1916 the British Salonika Force had very little to do except dig in.

At the beginning of October 1916, the Allies began another campaign to push forward into Serbia joined by the Greek army too. Success was eventually achieved towards the end of the war.

Salonika and Athens

Once at sea and away from Gallipoli we set a course for the island of Imbros and the harbour at Mudros, from where we had set sail in April. We were a sorry few, without horses, technical wagons, supplies or anything. We heaved a sigh of relief. At last it was over, and there was peace from the eternal shelling. Only nine of our original unit were left by then.

The harbour in Mudros was again full of ships, but this time there were many more hospital ships. Some nurses came out from a hospital marquee onto the shore as we sailed in and one of our boys shouted, 'Look, a woman!'. We hadn't seen one for 10 months, so we cheered.

We were at Mudros for a week when we were told we would be going to Salonika so we prepared and, in due course, we embarked and moved out of the harbour.

Submarines were active in the Mediterranean by then, and as we had a Battery of Field Artillery on board it was decided to mount four of their guns on the deck for additional defence. Two guns were mounted forward and two aft. They were placed to be able to fire from each corner of the ship, and lashed down onto to the rails and deck fittings. The long gun trails that really take the shock were put on heavy mats to help minimise the shock and protect the decking. We were all trained in the drill to fire the gun, and the next day our gun was fired for practice.

It went off all right, and so did the two men who sat on the trail. The gun jumped up in the air and all but went overboard with a deafening crash. The order 'cease fire' came and it was agreed to leave it until a submarine appeared.

One night I went on guard and submarine watch: two hours on, four off. It was a very dark night with nothing to be seen and only the swish of the propeller to be heard. It was so dark looking over the side one could just see the water. It would be difficult to see a submarine if one was about. We had just come off Gallipoli with its constant gunfire, and all this was very peaceful. It turned colder. I walked round looking at things in the dark as best I could, and opened the door of the ship's galley. Only a small room with ovens all down one side opposite one long table on which the bread was made and prepared for baking. I could smell home. Being in the warm I sat down and remembered no more until another member of the Guard shook me from my slumbers – it was light, 7am. I had not only slept my turn but the others as well. Because it had been a quiet night nothing was said. In point of fact, we all felt that a submarine watch at night was useless for it was well known that the submarines waited for daylight to attack. They had to see their targets to fire torpedoes

We sailed round the Greek islands for some time before arriving at Piraeus, the port for Athens. There we had to change ships. We embarked onto another boat, the *Queen Louise*. Scattered about in great disarray on our new ship we found guns of all sizes, horses and all types of wagons. Being interested in horses we wandered around the various decks looking them over. To our astonishment, nine of them were our horses mixed up with the others – and there was Timbuc! How he got there we never knew. When I left him on the beach at Gallipoli I had thought I would never see him again. We made a fuss of them all, and I started grooming and feeding Timbuc and spending time below.

From Athens we set off for Salonika but the authorities changed their minds and instead of Salonika we were told we were to go to France so, almost at Salonika, we turned back. In fact we did not know where we were going, for we sailed a zigzag course to baffle the submarines. After six weeks at sea we entered the harbour of Alexandria. Next day we disembarked and claimed our horses, which formed the nucleus of another company. What a fuss we made of them. In Alexandra we found an Army Corps of Cavalry, Indian troops, Australian light horse, our Infantry Battalions of the new Army recruited when war broke out.

There were something like 82,000 horses to feed with foodstuffs mostly from India. Once there we were regrouped and re-equipped in readiness for France and the Western Front. Once again things changed and instead I was told that I would be re-joining the General Headquarters Signal Company, which meant, for the time being, I was to stay in Egypt.

During the next period I was away a good deal because we had a mobile group whose job it was to rescue anyone stuck with a signal job they could not do. This took us on to the Western Libyan Desert to do communications for the 3rd Australian Light Horse Brigade[19] where the Senussids were causing trouble and also to the east to the Suez Canal.

---

[19]   Later my grandfather says this was the 5th Australian Light Horse Division.

171

The Western Libyan Desert and the Senussids

Egypt and the Western Libyan Desert showing the key towns in the war with the Senussids

The Senussids were an Islamic Order living in Libya and the Sudan. The scholar and teacher, the Grand Senussi, Sayyid Muhammad ibn Ali as-Senussi, had founded them in Mecca in 1837.

The Senussids had been involved, since the 1830's, in opposition to the colonisation of Algeria by the French and, in 1911-12, in opposition to the colonisation of Libya by the Italians.

Soon after the outbreak of war between Britain and Turkey, the Turkish government started to negotiate with them to gain their cooperation in the fight against the British. Within weeks of an agreement being reached, and under the command of Sayyid Ahmed ash-Sharif[20] the Senussids, together with other Berber tribesmen, began attacking the British. They also captured and held a group of British seamen and soldiers from two ships (*H.M.S. Tara* and the *S.S. Moorina*) that had been torpedoed off the North African coast by a German submarine.

By December 1915, the British had established a front in the Western Desert to repel the attacks – the Western Frontier Front – made up of the troops available in Egypt at that time. The result was a mixed bag of Australians, New Zealanders, South Africans, Indians, Sikhs, Ghurkhas, Egyptians and British troops from many different regiments and units. They were joined by a detachment from the Royal National Armoured Car Division led by the Duke of Westminster.

The first major encounter between these 'British' forces and the Senussids came towards the end of January 1916, but this was indecisive. The weather was bad and there was deep mud. All vehicles had to be dragged by soldiers and the armoured cars were useless in the attack.

In February, there was a more decisive result in a battle at Agagiya. The Senussids retreated 50 miles to the west of Sollum,

---

[20] His cousin Sayyid Idris later became King of Libya until the coup by Col. Gaddafi in 1969.

but the British commander decided to follow up the attack and to strike again as quickly as possible. The Duke of Westminster was ordered to chase them. In the pursuit the Duke's men captured all the enemy's guns and three Turkish officers.

Not satisfied with this victory, and with intelligence reports saying that the captured sailors and soldiers from the *Tara* and *Moorina* were being held within driving distance, the Duke set off to free them with 20 vehicles packed with infantry. They sped past the Sennussids, and on approaching the village the cars fanned out in a line and attacked the huts where the men were being held. The rescue was said to be surprisingly easy with no casualties. All the men were freed. It was said that despite being hungry, having lice and various fevers, they had been well treated.

The Duke of Westminster received the D.S.O. for what was described as a brilliant exploit. A report of the expedition appeared in all the newspapers in England and abroad, including the *New York Times*[21]. It was said to have provided the British public with some cheer and optimism during the dark days of fighting on the Western Front in France.

Meanwhile, in the British colony of Sudan to the south of Egypt, the Sultan of Darfur aligned himself with the Senussids. By May 1916, his army had risen to around 6,000 men, and the British sent a large force to engage them. In the ensuing battle the Sultan's forces didn't stand a chance against the machine guns and heavy artillery of the British and they were defeated.

Following the defeat there were no more full-on battles between the British and the Senussids. The tribesmen realised that they could

---

21 http://query.nytimes.com/mem/archive-free/pdf?res=F50A10F63E591A7A93CBA8178 8D85F428185F9

not win against heavy artillery and machine guns but they could do damage by reverting to their traditional methods of fighting – through raids on small forces and outposts. They re-organised and continued to attack the British whenever and wherever they could. They were to be a cause of much anxiety to the British commanders in Egypt until the end of the war.

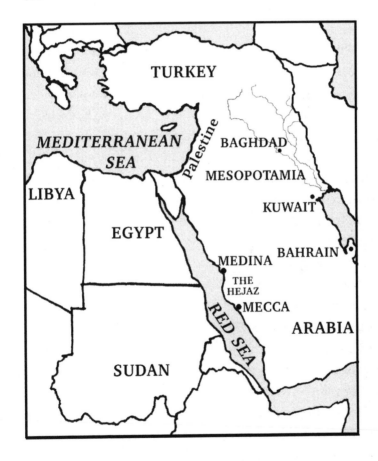

Egypt, Libya and the Sudan

No. 1 Field Punishment:
A Crime in Itself

We were loaned to the Australian 5th Light Horse Division, who were patrolling in the Western Libyan Desert where the Senussids were busy causing us trouble. We were needed for the signals since the Australian Division had no signals of their own. In the desert, in addition to the Australians there were also some English Infantry Units and the Duke of Westminster had an armoured car unit that was most unusual.

One morning, as we went out in the area of one of the Battalions of Infantry, we saw a soldier from one of the Regiments pegged out, with arms above his head and his legs spread apart. In other words, he was tied down, spread-eagled on the sand. He was undergoing what was called No.1 Field Punishment for a 'crime'. It was ordered by a Court Martial for what was regarded as a serious offence, for example refusing to obey an order or striking an NCO, etc. A Court Martial could order a man to be shot for cowardice, desertion etc. And No.1 Field Punishment was the next in descending order. Usually, the offenders were tied spread-eagled to a wagon wheel for so many hours each day.

We stopped to look at the poor chap. The Guard marched backwards and forwards with his rifle shouldered. We were asking what he had done to deserve this when a party of

Australians came up. They were amazed at the cruelty for they had no such thing in their Army. So, swearing loudly they told the Sentry to free him or they would. He said he had no power to do it and he would call the Orderly Officer. In due course, he came and tried to justify the punishment in a clever style but the Aussies told him bluntly that if the man wasn't freed they would do it and fasten the Officer down! So, with very bad grace, the Officer told the Guard to 'free the man' and take him to the Guardroom.

I only saw one other soldier tied to a gun wheel during the 1914-18 war but many were sentenced to imprisonment for cowardice and desertion. I acted as NCO in charge of tribunals once or twice. This brought home to me the freedom of the Australians and New Zealanders, whose ancestors left Britain for such crimes. I liked the way they dealt with injustice.

No.1 Field Punishment was subsequently abolished by Parliament. It should never have been used in a Civilian Army in wartime – nor indeed at any time. It shows the mentality of our rulers in the past.

Military Discipline in the First World War

Maintaining discipline in the Army was clearly an important matter. Small-scale misdemeanours were dealt with by the NCO's within the offender's unit. These were things like being late for parade, being untidy, not saluting etc. Punishments included losing a day's pay, extra exercise or being confined to barracks.

Moderately serious offences could either be dealt with by a district court martial or if a man preferred, by his commanding officer. Punishments here included detention for up to 28 days, forfeiting pay for 28 days, confinement to camp for up to two weeks, extra guard duty and field punishment.

Field Punishment No.1 involved the man being shackled in irons and secured to a fixed object, usually a gun wheel, for two hours in twenty-four and for not more than three days in four for up to twenty-one days. This was known by the troops as 'crucifixion'. Stories abounded of soldiers being positioned facing the enemy fire but allegedly out of range. There were also stories of soldiers being tied up so that they were suspended with their feet hardly touching the ground. In the heat of the desert, this punishment was particularly harsh. It was also harsh when the men had lice. It was eventually abolished in 1923.

Very serious crimes were all dealt with by a court martial. These included crimes that were tried in court in civilian life such as rape and murder and also military crimes such as desertion, striking a superior officer, negligently causing false alarms, and sleeping at your post when acting as a sentinel on active service – something my grandfather had been guilty of on the boat sailing to Salonika. The punishments for these crimes included penal servitude and death!

Back in Egypt: Eggs & Tomatoes

During our time in the region, we also worked on the railway telegraphs from Cairo to Bilbeis. In Egypt everything, or almost everything, could be bought in the street. As I have said before one of the most popular were the boys selling 'eggs a cook', boiled eggs that you could get at four for 1 piaster, a coin then worth tuppence in our money. They were very good food and nutritious. The eggs were small. The tomato sellers followed these boys. Their tomatoes were always big, and also four for 1 piaster. You can picture us walking along in our uniforms, egg in one hand and tomato in another.

We were puzzled at first by the Egyptian money but soon were used to it. There were a lot of small coins called milliemes but we never used them. I think they were metric so ten to one piaster The coinage was 1 piaster, 5 piastres, 10 piastres, 50 piastres (a paper note) and 100 piastres, also a note.

The poverty in Egypt was similar to that at home in Leeds, where many items were sold in the streets from baskets and barrows. In Leeds this was fish, oatcakes, yeast, milk, fruit and, in winter, roast chestnuts and potatoes. The unemployed in Leeds marched round the town regularly demonstrating about their conditions. Beggars were everywhere. Match sellers too. Strikes were frequent. To us in Leeds, talk of the wealth of the British Empire was a mockery and a farce. I did not believe in it and do not regret its end. Public schools provided the 'Administrators' in these territories and they enjoyed the wealth from the Empire, not us.

Cairo and Alexandria had a lot of open fronted street cafes, and a succession of beggars cadged their way round. They were very poor, some were good with tricks with corks and cards inviting customers to join them and guess the result.

Also at the horse races in Cairo the mature experts at the three-card trick were there in numbers with the police watching them carefully.

Perhaps the funniest thing I saw that demonstrated the Egyptian character to me was at the pigeon shooting: when the gunman fired, missed, and the bird fell – a winner, but the bird often did that I was told. It didn't pay to trust the people doing tricks for money too far – but we liked them.

While we were there, the 28th Division were ordered to Mesopotamia. General Townsend was surrounded in Kut-Al-Amara and likely to surrender, so a Relief Force was needed to go to his aid. The requisite troops were taken from Egypt. They sailed away to Bombay, to gather some more men there. Then we were told that we were to join them. I had learnt about Mesopotamia in our history lessons at school, so was quite looking forward to seeing the country of the Babylonians.

The War in Mesopotamia

Mesopotamia and its strategic location for the British Empire

Mesopotamia was the region between, and surrounding, the Tigris and Euphrates Rivers, now known as Iraq. It has a tremendous history. This was the land of the Babylonians and Noah's great flood. The Garden of Eden is said to have been located where the two rivers meet at Qurna.

When the war started in 1914, Mesopotamia was part of the Ottoman Empire, and was an area of extreme poverty. There were many different Arab groups living in and travelling through the region. The cities were very cosmopolitan. For example living in Basra were: Armenians, Indians, Arabs, Jews, Persians, Somalis, Ethiopians, British, French, Germans, Italians and Americans (mainly missionaries).

There was a thriving trade route through the region, and the British navy policed the waterways of the Persian Gulf to secure this trade (and later to secure the oil pipelines and refineries). But this was not an easy place to live with many diseases rife in the region including: smallpox, cholera, malaria and dysentery.

In 1901, a British entrepreneur, William Knox D'Arcy, who had made his fortune in the goldmines of Australia, negotiated the rights with local rulers to search for oil at the head of the Persian Gulf. He struck lucky in 1908, and from this emerged the Anglo-Persian Oil Company, APOC.

As war approached in 1914, Winston Churchill realised the need to secure the supplies of oil for the navy, which had been gradually replacing coal with oil as its principal fuel. Churchill gained government approval to purchase a controlling stake in APOC in August 1914, and later to purchase the company outright, forming British Petroleum (BP).

The British Raj, the colonial government in India, had responsibility for the Persian Gulf and, in August 1914, they were asked to draw up plans in case the Turks entered the war. The government in London wanted to protect the oil refinery at

Abadan. The British Raj had other fears. They were worried that if Turkey entered the war they may succeed in calling all Muslims to arms against the British in a holy war or jihad. With the large Muslim population in India, the British Raj took the view that the best way to prevent the spread of a jihad was to get as many of the Arab leaders in the Ottoman Empire to become allies of the British. Mesopotamia offered a way to do this.

The British already had allies in the region in the Sheikhs of Kuwait and Mohammerah. In India, the military planners thought the best way to gain Arab support was to send a force from India to the head of the Persian Gulf, even before war broke out with Turkey and the Ottoman Empire. The reasoning was that this would: a) tell the Turks that the British meant business; b) signal British support for the Arab leaders; and c) protect the oil installations. These plans were approved in September 1914. In the meantime, a British gunboat was sent up the Persian Gulf to join another one already there in some 'gunboat diplomacy'.

In October 1914, an Indian expeditionary force left Bombay for the Western Front. Half way across the Indian Ocean, the commander opened some sealed orders that he had been given on departure. These ordered him to sail into the Persian Gulf to protect British interests, and to be prepared to occupy Basra.

The ships arrived in the Persian Gulf on 23rd October 1914, before Turkey had entered the war. As a result, their arrival looked like a potential British invasion and they were not well received. In Bahrain they were told that the troops could not disembark. The soldiers had to stay on board, cooped up in hot, sweaty, cramped conditions.

Then, at the end of October 1914, Turkey declared its allegiance to the Central Powers, and entered war. The ships carrying the Indian Expeditionary Force were ordered north to the head of the Persian Gulf. They landed at Fao, easily taking the fort from the Turks.

There were few Turkish troops in Mesopotamia at that time and they were outnumbered and out-gunned by the British Indian Force. It is said that Basra was not so much captured by the British as abandoned by the Turks. During the brief fighting that took place it rained heavily and the British had a taste of what was to come. Almost immediately, the ground became a quagmire and the soldiers were ankle-deep in mud. Everything got stuck and nothing moved very quickly. They were fighting on a mud flat on the flood plain. The land was alternately a desert and a swamp.

The British took Basra on 23rd November 1914. The original aims of the mission had been achieved and, while the politicians and military hierarchy in London and India debated the next move, the British with their Indian troops began to take control of Basra and the surrounding area.

As the Turks left Basra they had taken all their papers or burnt them. All records of local land arrangements, tax collecting, indeed anything that would help the British administer the region disappeared. Whilst there was little resistance to the British occupation in Basra, the surrounding population on the land was hostile. Many Shia clerics in the holy cities joined the call to arms from the Sultan, and sent emissaries to the region to urge the local Arab leaders to join the jihad and fight the British. Britain's only weapon was bribery, which they used as they began to try to set up an administration including a police force.

The question was what to do next. Should the army stay put or go on to Baghdad? There were strong arguments for the army to keep moving up river towards Baghdad but many feared this would alienate more of the Arab population. Political disagreements ensued between London and India about whether this should be an offensive or defensive campaign.

Eventually it was decided to sail up to Qurna at the junction of the Tigris and Euphrates, and the town was taken with minimal fighting on the 9th December 1914. The Turks then retreated 100 miles further up the river, and a number of local Arab leaders turned against the Turks. This dashed any hopes the Turks had of an organised jihad against the British throughout the region but did not assuage the fears of the British in India about a Muslim uprising there.

During the period of the landings on Gallipoli in April and May 1915, the arguments about the mission in Mesopotamia repeated – should they stay in Qurna or push on to Amara? The history books describe General Nixon, commander of the forces in the region, as an optimist and General Townsend, who led the forces in Qurna, as one of the most reckless individuals in the British Army. With no reinforcements, Nixon told Townsend to push on to Amara.

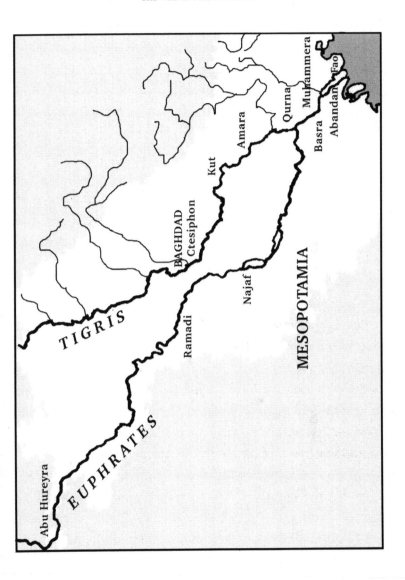

Mesopotamia and key towns in the war to take Baghdad

Amara was taken without firing a shot, on 31st May 1915.

The British supply lines were becoming thin. They were entirely reliant on water transport up the River Tigris, and with the river silting up with the floods, and with a shortage of small supply boats, it was becoming harder to maintain the force the further they went up river. It was even harder to evacuate the wounded – it took hours to reach Basra but mission creep had set in. Townsend was told that he may have to go to Kut, but no further. He argued that they should stay in Amara whilst the Gallipoli campaign was in the balance. He lost the argument. The journey to Kut was hard. Supply ships ran aground, and men had to walk in the heat. They had no tents and often no food. Nevertheless, the British took Kut at the end of September 1915.

After the fighting, the troops suffered from heat exhaustion, thirst and hunger. There were no medical services; men lay where they fell for hours on end. The conditions for those that were shipped back to Basra were indescribable.

Townsend led the forces he had left, and tried to follow the Turks up the river. His aim was to capture them with their guns as they retreated, but he failed. This left a sizeable Turkish force in Baghdad with much better supply routes than the British.

The arguments began again as to whether to stay put or to move on to capture Baghdad. At this point, the fear of defeat in Gallipoli entered the equation. In London, Kitchener argued that the army should stay on Gallipoli so the Turks could not send reinforcements to Mesopotamia. Churchill argued that if Baghdad was not captured then Persia (now Iran) may join the Turks, particularly if the Allies evacuated Gallipoli. After much debate the decision was taken to push on to Baghdad, if nothing else it would divert attention from Gallipoli.

General Townsend needed reinforcements but they took time to arrive. He moved up river to Ctesiphon in November 1915, but this time the Turkish forces were ready. They had regrouped and prepared. When he realised the battle was lost, General Townsend gave the order to retreat. As soon as the Turks saw that the British forces were leaving, they set off to chase them. The British retreated to Kut, where the Turks encircled the fort and a siege began on 7th December 1915.

In the New Year of 1916, after the British evacuation from Gallipoli, the Turks moved their troops to reinforce their lines in Mesopotamia. The British made several attempts to relieve the siege of Kut. In the first battle in January 1916 the British losses were estimated at 19,000 men, killed or wounded. More troops were sent from Egypt, including my grandfather. They sailed up the Tigris to Basra, and some went on to Amara to join the fighting to relieve the siege.

Supplies were dropped by plane into Kut but after four months things became desperate. The soldiers were starving, and many were ill.

Attempts were made to negotiate the end of the siege with two agents sent to talk to the Turks – including T.E. Lawrence (Lawrence of Arabia) – but before the talks were concluded Townsend surrendered on 29th April 1916.

The surrender, coming soon after the evacuation from Gallipoli, was seen as one of the worst military disasters the British had ever suffered. It was a blow to British prestige in the region but the fears of it leading to an uprising in the Muslim world, particularly in India, did not come to pass.

British forces moved back to Amara. The new arrivals from Egypt re-embarked and sailed back to Egypt to join the campaign in Palestine and elsewhere.

The Turks took General Townsend to an island in the Sea of Marmara where he saw out the war in relative luxury. His men, on the other hand, were marched to Baghdad and many were put to work on the Berlin to Baghdad railway. Thousands died.

It would be a year before there was another attempt by the British to take Baghdad.

A Radio Station that Could Communicate with the Eiffel Tower

The 12th Division was ordered to Mesopotamia, and we went with them via Bombay, Karachi and the Persian Gulf to Basra. This was the land between the two rivers, the Tigris and Euphrates, associated with the Assyrian and Babylonian dynasties. I had read all about their history when I was a child. The huge public library was another advantage of living in Leeds. I liked reading, and went as often as I could. I read quickly, and had about five books a week. I only had one complaint though, a book could not be returned on the same day that it was borrowed. I would get a book and go down into the art gallery below and read it but I had to keep it until the next day. I read all G.A. Henty's books and those of Charles Kingsley, Fergus Hume, and Dickens. Books took me on voyages all around the world and even under the sea.

We went up the river Tigris on barges, so had no shelter from the Turks firing from the banks, it was all very hostile. Also, we had a large number of men sick. The river water was dirty, quite unfit for drinking, even for washing really and those who drank it without purification soon fell ill. Unfortunately no Royal Army Medical Corps (R.A.M.C.) units were included in the Campaign so our ill and wounded had to be cared for by our men. Some came with us up river whilst others were sent back to India. A good number died of course.

General Townsend had to capitulate before we got there, and he and his troops were taken prisoners and marched to Aleppo and Turkey – another badly arranged adventure. He was expected to fight, and he had no medical unit with him either. They had to carry their wounded on with them or leave them where they fell. So our mission was unsuccessful, and we returned to Egypt to get ready for the crossing of the Sinai Desert.

Whilst we were in Basra, one of our men built a radio station capable of sending messages to the Eiffel Tower – the first radio station in that part of the world. I put down an earth a mile long – buried (it was a No.8 standard wire gauge).

Then we went back to Egypt again and we went on leave in Cairo, where we stayed at the Bristol Hotel. I have always looked around for history and geography, and three of us paid a guide, then £1 per day plus meals and travel, to show us around. We saw all the sights in Cairo and round about, going as far as Luxor, down into some of the burial rooms where the walls were covered with hieroglyphics and into the Pyramids. Truly the ancients were remarkable builders. By contrast the present Egyptian peasant seemed less remarkable, at least those in our working parties, but then our work was less remarkable than the Pyramids!

Working with the Egyptians, I gradually acquired a working knowledge of Arabic. At school I had liked languages: French, Latin and German. I won the Latin prize one year, and had a distinction in German in another. English, of course, presented no difficulty thanks to my beloved sister, who taught it as well as geography and history. There were 25 approximately in each form at school, and since I had a good memory I was usually in the first four.

The Suez Canal:
That Precious Pipeline

Once Gallipoli was evacuated, the Turks moved their forces towards the Suez Canal. It was estimated that they would have up to 200,000 men there by early 1916. The defence of the canal became a top priority for the British.

Before the evacuation, it had been decided that the British forces from Gallipoli would move to defend the canal and General Archibald Murray was appointed to organise this. The assembled British Forces included troops from Australia, New Zealand, India, Egypt and many other British colonies at that time.

The British began to build defensive structures all along the canal. A narrow gauge railway was also built to bring in supplies from Egypt, together with a pipeline that provided drinking water from the Nile.

In April 1916, Turkish troops were reported in the region, 25 miles from the canal in Sinai. The British attacked but were driven back. Later that same day, the Turks withdrew – they described the battle as more of a reconnaissance mission.

By early June 1916, the British had moved up into Sinai to extend the defensive cover to the canal. They occupied the town of Romani with very little resistance.

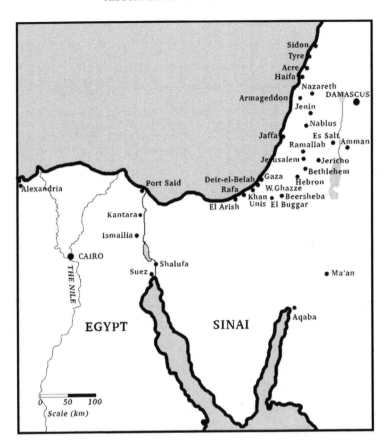

Suez, Sinai and Palestine

Some Extreme Swimming

View of Kantara across the Suez Canal

Back in Egypt we were with GHQ Signals, and spent time at HQ. Then we were posted to Ismailia. We started work along the Suez Canal, establishing communications at various selected stations from Port Said, Ballah, Shalufa down to the town of Suez where defences were being constructed. Our base was in Ismailia, half way down the canal. I used to swim across regularly, sometimes twice each day, on the outward and inward journeys from our base. The wagon went on the ferry; I undressed and swam it. The current down the canal was quite strong, and around Ismailia there was continual traffic – the tugs and barges moved fairly fast so it was quite a challenge but I enjoyed it.

One day, one of our boys, Baxter, said he would like to swim with me, and so I explained the tactics to him. We both dived in. I swam quickly and, arriving at the pontoon across, I looked round. To my surprise there was a string of barges going down and he was on one so I waved to him to come and he dived in. I went to meet him, and when we came ashore he said I left him in the middle and he saw the barges coming fast. They were passing. He was afraid of being run down. One had a rope trailing, which he grabbed on to, and the speed pulled him up on board! He didn't try it again. Once I tried swimming under a ship passing down the Canal but never repeated it. I had to go down a long way and seemed to be under the water for quite a long time. When I emerged on the other side of the ship, I rose to the surface so rapidly that I almost leapt out of the water. Quite frightening.

On one of our visits back in Alexandria I went down to the Cleopatra Depot for a sports competition. I won 2 of the swimming races. Ladies were present at the competition, so I needed a costume, something that covered me up. I was lent a silk one, which I thought was very posh.

Norman at the Cleopatra Depot

Riding along the bank of the Suez Canal from Ballah to Ismailia was often at the beginning or end of a working party when the redoubts were being made to repel any possible Turkish invasion from the East. One day there were several ships going through the canal from Port Said to Suez. They were big ships, twin funnelled, from various shipping lines, and their size brought their upper decks level with the bank of the canal. They always proceeded slowly, about five miles an hour, so as not to injure the banks, which were, of course, all sand. I watched them with interest and I suppose they did with me.

Suddenly, from the same level as me there was a shout 'Eh Woodcock!', and I looked in the direction of the voice. There was a soldier waving his arms and jumping on the deck. I recognised him as a Lance Corporal who trained with us in England, so I asked where they were going. 'To Mesopotamia' came the reply. So I rode along, and we held quite a conversation as the boat sailed steadily along. It seemed so incongruous, he on a liner and me on shore so many miles from home. Then we waved goodbye – I never saw him again, so I don't know if he survived the Campaign and returned, but I imagine if he did he would recite the story from the ship. He was surprised, and so was I.

In Ismailia the horses had good food, plenty of sand to roll in and a salt-water lake, Lake Timsah, to swim in. They enjoyed it, and we did too. Their coats shone and they became frisky again. I had taught Timbuc to lie down and also to come when I called or whistled. One day when I had been out with a working party, as we came back to the lines I saw him harnessed as the off lead horse in a six horse team. The driver looking after him tried him in harness to see what he would do. Bless me, when I saw him I laughed. He was so eager to pull his weight that he might have been the only one to work, he pressed forward into the collar as if he liked it, not like most of the horses that would buck and jib at the strange restriction of it. He was quite a pet with the drivers, all of them being pleased to look after him with their own.

During this period, the three of us (Jones, Wilkinson and me, Woodcock) were sent to man an outpost from where we would patrol regularly in different directions and report anything suspicious. At this post, we had a dugout with four steps down into it. Rations and water came up every four days by camel. It was known as 'Half Way Post' near Kantara. The daily patrols involved long journeys for the horses, so much so that one by one they grew very tired and had to be replaced. One lasted a month, one five weeks. Timbuc lasted six weeks. He went very thin and lost all his sparkle, and so he was taken back. In his place I had a big horse, a roan, standing 17 hands. By comparison he was slow and, after a fortnight, returning from a patrol one day he just lay down. There was I, still on his back, with my feet on the ground, and he refused to move until I got off. When he stood up, I remounted and he promptly went down again. So I had to walk and lead him in. Following that incident we were relieved and I returned to Timbuc; we were pleased to see each other again. I bought him a sting of figs at the canteen.

Horses did not like camels and, until they grew accustomed to them, they would shy and career away. Jones and I were riding along the bank up the Sweet Water Canal from the Nile to near Ballah when several camels appeared. Our horses raised their ears, looked in their direction and grew restive. When they came near to pass, Jones's horse took a flying leap into the canal and swam across. After the camels had passed he said, 'What do I do now, I'm on the wrong side?' There were no bridges. So I said, 'Well, you are wet now, so make him swim back.' Jones could not swim so he just remained in the saddle, and it was warm, very warm, so we rode on and he dried off.

We had telephone communication with GHQ in Ismailia. The three of us worked well together. We took turns on the patrols and shared other duties, like cooking. All we saw were Arabs on sandhills in the distance who disappeared before we got to them. But we had to keep a close eye at all times, at night in particular, because in the desert the Arabs knew the areas. They were noted thieves, not above killing to rob.

The Night Attack

One night we were woken up by noises outside and the sound of someone coming down the dugout steps. Wilkinson had a bed on the left of the doorway (which had a sack for privacy), Jones had his bed on the right and I was across the other side opposite the entrance. Wilkie called out, 'Who is there?' There was a sound of footsteps running up the steps. Then they came back again. As we all had our rifles ready, I said I would fire one round at the doorway if they returned. Mine was the safest place from which to fire. Then we heard a scraping outside and again someone coming down so I sighted my rifle and, I should say, I held it in a position to hit the doorway and pulled the trigger. There was a loud bang and a rushing of feet up the steps and a gurgle of liquid. I said it sounded as if I had hit whoever it was and Wilkie struck a match and lit the candle. The gurgling continued and I thought the visitor must be bleeding to death. The light of the candle revealed that I had pierced our tank of water, our four days supply. I jumped out of my blankets and tilted it to stop the flow. Next day, we found our visitor, it was a mongoose, an animal that can kill a snake; we had some big snakes about and could have used him if we had captured him. We were short of water until the next delivery arrived, but we were always short of water and became used to the thirst.

The mongoose wasn't the only animal we had around us; there were quite a lot of wild donkeys about at that spot around our dugout. Donkeys and camels were the beasts of burden, and these were the escapees. Removing manure somewhere further away from our dugout was necessary, so we decided to catch one of the donkeys and use that, putting a partly filled sack across its back. We spent two days catching one. They were wily. We had a 15-foot rope with one man at each end. We managed to run it around the donkey's legs and bingo, we had him.

All went happily at first, but he had lived in the wild on nothing much. We gave him oats and bran and his output became more than our three horses. He had never had it so good and revelled in it. So, reluctantly, we put him back in the wild, but he kept coming back and helped himself by bursting our feed sacks. So we moved them but he never left us and continued to visit our successors. Being horsemen, we were fond of animals.

After a time, our rations at the outpost grew poorer. We asked for eggs and tomatoes, as we knew they were plentiful, for which we would pay. Supplies were brought, but more than we needed. We were there some months and then we were told we would be relieved. We looked around our dug out and found we had 54 eggs in stock. We could not carry them in addition to all our equipment. So, what to do with them? We started the day with four each as 'Bombay Oysters[22]', eight each fried for breakfast and the rest in a stew at mid-day. We were all quite well and ready to move off soon after lunch.

Stealing Timbuc Back

Soon we had to learn to ride camels. We were to cross the Sinai Desert to Palestine, chasing the Turks away from the canal. Timbuc returned to the Ismailia camp during this period so the drivers had him to themselves to look after. They were pleased but I wasn't; I was not fond of riding camels.

Eventually, we got to Gaza and I was transferred to the 1st Heavy Artillery Brigade as a Sergeant. I asked that Timbuc be transferred too but was refused as my OC was taking him in a second mount. So I said good bye again.

Some time later, after we had made progress into Palestine, we were camped for several days in one place. We were out on patrol regularly, and one day one of my men said, 'Sergeant Major, your old mob have come up the line and are here by the railhead.' I knew Timbuc would be with them, my best friend, so I said to him, 'Tonight when it falls dark saddle my horse, you are going with me for another.' Off we went together in the dark carefully finding our way between the tents and the supplies. Eventually, he showed me where they were, GHQ Signals. Quietly, I walked along the picket line until I found Timbuc. Softly I said his name and his head went up. I put my arm around his neck and whispered, 'Quiet boy, I have come

---

22   A glass of water with a dash of vinegar and a raw egg floating on top. You have to drink it without breaking the egg yolk.

for you.' As he settled, I started untying the head rope. Then a voice rang out, 'Halt, who goes there?' He was the Guard, with rifle cocked.

So I called to him, 'Woodcock here.'

'We were expecting you and the OC said if Woodcock called he wanted to see him.'

'Where is he?' I asked.

'In that hut over there.'

I went and knocked. That was the Officers' Mess. The doors opened and the light was upon me.

'It's OK Woodcock. I have decided you can have him,' the OC said. I was surprised but he said, 'I knew you would come for him sometime.'

So I thanked him and we set off for our lines, me patting Timbuc every now and then. I was delighted to have him back again. Champion!

Norman on Timbuc, Ismailia 1916

Through the Sinai Desert to the Border with Palestine

In July 1916, the British had 14,000 men in the region around Romani to the east of the Suez Canal. This was the most that the water pipeline could supply. In August, the Turks launched a major offensive against them, and the Battle of Romani took place. After five days of fighting, the Turks were beaten back and retreated to El Arish.

The battle of Romani was the last attempt by the Turks to take the Suez Canal. Following this, General Archibald Murray moved his headquarters back to Cairo, which did not go down well with the troops, especially since it was in The Savoy Hotel.

The British then advanced on El Arish. The go ahead for the advance was given but with the proviso that the advance did not outpace the railway or the water pipeline. The existing pipeline was insufficient for the number of men required for the fighting, so another larger gauge pipe was laid which reached Romani in mid-November. By 7th December 1916, the pipe and the railway had reached Mazar (see map), and the British advance could resume.

At this point a new Allied force was constituted, the Desert Column, and they began forays to the outskirts of El Arish. At the same time, the Imperial Camel Brigade was formed.

In London, David Lloyd George had just been appointed prime minister, and he took a personal interest in the campaign in the

Middle East, making it clear that he wanted the Turks expelled from Jerusalem. Murray was asked to advance through El Arish and on into Palestine. He promised to do this and to take the town of Rafa with the troops he had available.

Murray gave the order to advance on El Arish on 20th December 1916. Aerial reconnaissance indicated that the Turks had retreated out of the town. Australian and New Zealand forces took it easily. The Turks were then pursued to the southeast. Water had to be carried for the troops and their animals by camel, which slowed down the Allied Forces as they went in pursuit.

Eventually, the Turks were encountered in Magdhaba and fighting began. The commander of the Allied force in the battle was contemplating a withdrawal due to the lack of water and supplies. However, just as he was about to issue the command to withdraw, the Australian and New Zealand forces broke through the Turkish lines and soon the fighting was over and almost 1,300 Turkish troops were taken prisoner.

The relative ease with which the Allies had taken El Arish and Magdhaba encouraged the commanders to ask Murray for permission to go on towards Rafa without waiting for the railway and pipeline to be built. Patrols were sent out for reconnaissance. The landscape beyond El Arish changed from the desert to more countryside with cultivated crops, water supplies and reasonable roads. The Light Car Patrol could now be used in the advance. Murray said 'yes' and the troops moved forward on 8th January 1917.

Rafa was then a small village with a keep of a medieval castle on a hill nearby. The keep and the hill were well defended by the Turks, and fighting went on all day. By late afternoon the commander, the same one who had been contemplating a withdrawal during the battle for Magdhaba, once more began contemplating giving the command to withdraw. Again, before he had chance to issue the command the Antipodean troops charged and penetrated the Turkish defences, taking the central redoubt using bayonets. With that, the Turkish resistance collapsed and Rafa was in the hands of the Allies.

The Turkish forces withdrew north to Gaza and Beersheba. The British were now at the gateway to Palestine.

Sand and Camels in the Desert

As the march forward from Kantara began, we moved up and opened Signal Offices at the railhead. A full gauge track was being laid together with permanent telegraph lines and a 12-inch water main to carry water across the desert to supply our forces as we advanced. A pontoon bridge spanned the canal to carry the train and the pipeline.

The route of the railway and the pipeline followed the ancient track from Egypt through Palestine, Syria and Turkey to Russia. The Eastern Telegraph Company had operated this route before the Great War and, because of wood-eating insects, all the poles over the desert were bolted to iron plates that were sunk into the sand. The plates were about a foot wide and helped during the Khamsin (the hot, dry wind that blows in this part of the world, carrying great quantities of sand) by resisting the wind. As the railway progressed, there were places where it crossed under the telephone lines, and so temporary poles were erected that were longer and thinner to take the wires over the train. These had to be replaced ultimately by stouter ones, and we were given the job of repairing any broken lines.

Imagine the position. Sand stretched for miles in all directions, not a soul about there, just sand disturbance where digging had occurred and the railway line stretching East and West with nothing on it. We unloaded our gear from camels and started

208

by adding guy lines to stretch the sagging poles, and then we replaced the mangled wire across the railway, which had been caught by a passing engine. While our man was working up above, making the lines secure, there was a whistle and a train appeared puffing out a cloud of black smoke. It ran straight underneath our boy and he had to hang on tightly or he would have been blown off.

After the train had passed with driver and fireman waving, our lad came down. He was just covered in black soot. So we rolled him in the soft sand for some time, then brushed him down, but he was just as black as soot – and swearing like a trooper! It reminded me of a time at home in Cudworth. We had just moved into a new house on Barnsley Road. At that time there was no gas or electricity, only oil lamps and candles. A paraffin lamp was in the bathroom and one morning it smoked. When my sister Annie went in to wash, she came out covered in black cobwebs. She didn't get to school that morning.

Our thirst was tremendous. It was truly awful. Our water ration was limited to half a gallon per man per day (4 pints)[23]. In the desert a man could drink a quart (2 pints) at one go and our tongues cleaved to the roofs of our mouths. Death by thirst must be terrible.

There was no water for miles, and we had the barest minimum from the pipeline we built. This was Nile water via Kantara. The railway and pipeline followed us as we moved up country. Nile water ultimately flowed into Jerusalem. The brackish water occasionally found in the desert was useless, undrinkable. Our

---

[23] Current military guidelines for drinking water for soldiers in the desert advise at least a pint of water per man per hour and up to 3 pints per hour in the high heat of the day.

horses suffered from thirst too, and many died. That was our main difficulty as we moved on.

One day we had to go to the railhead for supplies, on camels, and lo and behold at the railhead was an engine with steam in it. We gathered round, and under the cab step was a trickle of hot water. In no time, we were undressed and all having a wash, our first for weeks. The engine driver overstayed his time, and before leaving we all had a drink out of his tank. It tasted of oil but went down as nectar! Whenever I closed my eyes I dreamt of water – the cold water in the Dales that we had played in during our school camp. We went potholing down Gaping Gill, but at the time I did not care for climbing about the wet caves and up through waterfalls. I was better at swimming in the rock pools on top. Although it was summer, the temperature of the water as it came from the caves was only 45° so we took a breath, dived in, and across, then out. One breath. Never one for climbing, on the second day, which was very warm and sunny, I lay on the grass on my back and watched as my friends struggled up the steep slopes. It was a wonderful holiday.

Water supplies to working parties in the desert were vital and, at this time, became later and later in arriving, despite all our protests. And we did protest. Tempers were often frayed and one day I had enough and said I would give up working until the water arrived. The others all followed suit and we downed tools. I was ordered to continue but refused, so was put under arrest. I was marched back to our lines and charged with disobeying an order – a serious charge for which I knew I could be shot or sent to prison for months.

The charge was reduced by our OC to 'not complying with an order' so that he could deal with it – I was needed for the signals work. The OC said he had just recommended me for promotion and was very disappointed. He banished me on a one-man patrol for a month – not altogether pleasant but it could have been much worse. After a fortnight, I was brought back because I was missed and there was more important work to do. I was 19 years-old then. Perhaps rather hot headed (or touched by the sun). In due course my promotion to Lance Corporal (paid) came from England.

The Turks, in the meantime, struggled across the Sinai Desert as far as Romani where, in April 1916, they were conclusively beaten, and they began to fall back towards Palestine. Before the battle of Romani we did the signal work for the 3rd Australian Light Horse Brigade, as they had no signals of their own.

Once the Turks began to fall back, we were in a position to follow them up. We worked our way to Mazar, through about 8 kilometres of loose sand which drifted in the hot dry winds making hills one day and shifting them another. Living in a desert is uncomfortable, and it was very hot in the Sinai Desert in 1916. You long for shade and there is none, and it becomes harassing. Blood becomes thin and watery. You can cut yourself and not bleed. Sores are common too, the skin, being dry, punctures easily and usually goes septic. Many times you could see a battalion of men all with bandages on some part of their body.

The Turks made several stands and fought hard, but unsuccessfully, and we eventually reached the Wadi Ghazze, which was the border with Palestine.

Of Men, Mutiny and Revolution

After Rafa was captured in January 1917, preparations were made to advance into Palestine and take Gaza.

In Russia the 'February Revolution' took place, and this brought fear to the Allies of the Russian front collapsing, allowing the Germans to pull their troops back and into France.

In March, General Maude captured Baghdad so there was some good news in London. His forces then began to move towards Palestine to join with the British Forces, including my grandfather, who were advancing north from Sinai.

In early April, the Americans joined the war and the fighting. This has been described as 'realpolitik' since there was a realisation in the USA that if they wanted to influence the decisions about the division of land after the war ended, for example in the Middle East, then they had to be involved in the fighting. The resumption of German submarine attacks in the Atlantic also contributed to their decision to join the war.

In April 1917, the Allies launched a spring offensive in France – the Nivelle Offensive. This saw the British engaged in the Battle of Arras and the French further south at St Quentin. The offensive was planned to end the war in a short space of time by breaking through German defences where they were thought to be at their weakest. When the battle ended, the Allies had made significant advances but had failed to break the German lines.

After the Nivelle Offensive, French soldiers began to mutiny. Thousands left the frontline, and many refused to return to the trenches believing the attacks they were being asked to make were futile. The mutinies were kept secret but historians record that more than half the divisions in the French army were involved. In June 1917, the French authorities took action with mass arrests and court martials. Over 500 men were sentenced to death (less than 50 were actually shot). Others were sentenced to hard labour.

As a result of the mutiny, longer and more regular leave was introduced for all troops and there were less 'grand' offensives where the soldiers climbed out of the trenches to face German guns. With the Americans joining the war, more and better tanks appeared on the Western Front reducing the need for such attacks. This happened at the time when the news of the Russian Revolution was reaching the troops, which worried the authorities in both France and Britain.

The Advance Into Palestine: The First Battle of Gaza

March, 1917

We had pushed our way across the Sinai Desert from Kantara on the Suez Canal to El Arish (the place where Methuselah was buried) with the Desert Mounted Corps. Later, their title was changed to 'Eastforce'.

We proceeded to Rafa for the first attack on Gaza. We were a section of General Headquarters Signals. Rafa was where the desert ended and soil began so, from then on, thank goodness, horses succeeded camels. From there we advanced at night with Infantry and Cavalry Patrols screening our front, the battle being timed to commence early in the morning.

In the 100-mile long trek across the sandy desert, we fought several engagements and suffered continually from thirst and lack of decent food. We continued to lose many of our animals from lack of water. High Command was in Cairo, 200 miles away and seemed to know nothing of our difficulties. We wondered how it was possible for an Army Commander to manage his forces from such a distance. We heard of him, Sir Archibald Murray, but, of course, never saw him, neither did he ever see us. Our stock phrase was: 'Archi, bold? – certainly not!'

To make things easier from a signals point of view, we prepared a wagon as a Signal office with telegraph equipment all wired up inside, the sides being of timber and rush matting. It looked a queer contraption and, so far as we were aware, had not been used elsewhere. Presumably, all we had to do was to connect up the lines we had brought with us from Egypt and bring in those from the Divisions engaged in the coming battle.

1.5kW Marconi wireless set mounted on a wagon, 1916.
Photo courtesy of the Royal Signals Museum

For the Gaza battle, we had to move at night with Cavalry and Infantry Patrols as cover. No one knew the country and evidently we outstripped our Patrols. Suddenly, in the night, we were surrounded by a large Turkish Patrol and they were as surprised as we were by their sudden appearance. We were captured.

The Turks were so interested in our Signal office contraption that they spent time looking into and over it. Obviously, they did not know what it was for. They had no idea that a battle was imminent, or that we had so many troops moving up and, thinking they had plenty of time, they did not hurry in their search. They were caught unaware when a voice called: 'Halt, who goes there?', and before long were surrounded by a Patrol of our boys who swarmed over us. We were free; the Turks were prisoners. Had the Turks known that they had captured the main HQ Signal Office they would, indeed, have marched it back to their lines with glee. We were considerably relieved, and moved forward to our allotted map location and prepared for the action to start.

Next day the battle commenced. Fighting became confused. We spent time trying to find one of our Divisions and when we did, about 4pm, the first order was 'to return'. We did, to the Wadi Ghazze, and that day our dead and wounded were 12,000. We would have been captured but for the fact that the enemy also retired. The Turks came back next day. We prepared for the next attack. Sir Archibald Murray the Commander-in-Chief was, as usual, in his Headquarters in Cairo. He never ventured out during the Campaign.

Just before dawn, the first rifle fire broke out, followed by the rattle of machine guns and Artillery shelling. We accepted the Divisional and other telephone lines and connected them up as events began to happen. Our troops were held up on a ridge to the east of Gaza. Casualties were mounting. The Turks were entrenched in prepared positions that, apparently, we did not know about.

The battle went on, with reports coming in. Then, at 10am, came the cry: '54th Division out of communication. Send out

216

a party to find them as quickly as possible.' I was one of the party. We went forward to Samson's Ridge (this was the biblical Samson who brought down the gates of Gaza) but the Division Headquarters had been shelled out of there and no one knew where they had gone. We searched around the countryside and, eventually, found them at 4pm, when we contacted Eastforce and informed them of the position. In fact, for a large part of the day, the 54th Division, brigades and Battalions, had been out of communication. The first order received was to retire to the Wadi Ghazze, about two miles south, and prepare a defence. As we were a separate unit, we made ready to return immediately but the Officer commanding the 54th Division Signals, stepped up and insisted that we retire with his Company (I think he must have felt important having GHQ Signals with him).

During the night, he got lost and decided we must wait until daylight. As we stood by, everything seemed to go past us: guns, Infantry, Cavalry and then the battlefield fell quiet. Daylight came and we resumed our retreat, to be later challenged by a Sentry: 'Halt, who goes there?' The Major rode towards him and replied: '54th Divisional Signal Company.' The Sentry said: 'Oh – we are the Rearguard, you have been out in front all night then,' which meant, of course, that if the Turks had come forward, we would have been taken prisoner. We reported the Major for preventing us from joining our unit and Eastforce. Subsequently, we heard that he was demoted and sent back to England.

The casualties on that day amounted to 18,000 according to our messages by way of Signals to GHQ. The English newspapers in their reports gave the numbers as 9,000. This seemed to be usual practice at that time, to halve the losses!

One innovation in that battle was not used again. The Infantry had pieces of tin fastened to the equipment on their backs. The idea was that the sun would glint on them and show our Artillery observers just where they were. Unfortunately, when a man was killed he often spun around, and the enemy then knew exactly where the rest of his men were and turned the guns directly onto them.

One of the saddest sights I ever saw was on the morning after the retreat when the Battalions paraded for inspection. The first one I watched had only 24 men on parade. I knew from past experience how they felt, having lost so many comrades.

One reason why we were not captured on the night of the retreat was because the Turks also had so many casualties that they retreated from their positions and it was about 2am the next day when they discovered we had gone, so they came back and occupied their previous positions.

We repaired our losses and prepared for another attack, which took place a month later. The result was the same but this time we occupied the ground from the Mediterranean Sea on our left, across the front of Gaza towards Beersheba and the desert.

The Dangers of the Desert

For the troops living in trenches in this part of the world it was an altogether different experience to that of the troops on the Western Front in France and Belgium. In the desert there were snakes, scorpions, tarantulas and all manner of insects not seen before. There were frequent sandstorms and goggles had to be worn when issued. Often soldiers worked with handkerchiefs tied over their noses and mouths to keep the sand out. It stuck to them when they perspired, got into almost every mouthful of food they ate and into the water too. With so little water, keeping clean was a problem too.

Health problems included sunburn and dry and cracked skin, no doubt made worse by the lack of water to drink. Dust got into sores that then became septic. Even sitting in the saddle of a horse or a camel could be painful. Health problems were added to when the temperature swung from the high heat of the desert during the day to almost freezing at night.

The soldiers suffered from many diseases and illnesses, not least cholera that came from drinking water from contaminated wells.

Sandfly fever, or three-day fever, as it was known, was prevalent at certain times of the year. It is an acute infectious feverish disease transmitted to humans by the blood sucking female sandfly. In the Middle East it breaks out in epidemic form during the summer season following sandfly breeding. Once infected, it takes between two and a half to five days for symptoms to appear when there is suddenly a feeling of complete fatigue and lethargy, combined with stomach ache and dizziness, followed within one day by the chills and a rapid rise in pulse and temperature for one or two days. Symptoms can also include severe headaches with pain behind the eyes and intense muscular and joint pains. Usually, after two days the temperature slowly returns to normal and only rarely is there a second episode of fever. Following this, the patient will feel great fatigue and weakness, accompanied by slow pulse and, frequently, very low blood pressure. Convalescence may require a few days or several weeks, but the prognosis is always good. There is no specific treatment other than to treat each symptom as it appears.

With water coming from a pipeline from the Nile, inevitably it was rationed. In preparation for the third battle for Gaza, the planners realised that they needed the troops to be able to march at night and on very low water rations, since the water had to be carried. They needed the horses on low water rations too. As a result the men were 'trained' to live on 2 pints per day. Horses were similarly trained to manage on less water. Night marching was practiced until it was felt that the troops could travel further and on less water than the Turks would anticipate.

Struck Down by a Mystery Fever, April, 1917

We moved up to Deir el-Belah to prepare for the second battle for Gaza, which was to be on a bigger scale than the previous one. Additional batteries of heavy Artillery arrived, and we had quite a big programme of work in preparation.

Suddenly, men started to become sick. In the morning, on first parade at 6am, they were, apparently, quite well but by breakfast time they suddenly collapsed and were almost unconscious. We took them to the Casualty Clearing Station, a marquee with stretchers for beds and one blanket. The doctors were at first puzzled by the symptoms and, indeed, so were we when more and more went.

We had so many horses to water, feed, groom and exercise and one man could not look after more than three at one time, and there were all the other duties that could not be left. However, the numbers of men going sick kept rising, until only seventeen of us were left.

Then, one morning, I took the first parade, went to get water for a wash and collapsed. When I came to I was in the Field Ambulance. I was anxious to know what would happen to the Unit because the only NCO left was a Second Corporal, and the number of men was quite insufficient. I had never been sick in this situation before and wondered what the result would be. However, I was really in no fit state to bother about anything.

The next day I persuaded myself that the pills the R.A.M.C. gave me were doing their job, and I implored the doctor not to send me down the line to a base hospital. At the end of a week I asked to be discharged. The doctor said, 'If you can walk through the doorway we will think about it.' So I stood up and immediately fell down. Why, I don't know. No one had ever seen a sandfly, so what they were like I cannot say, and whether there were such things was also a mystery. Incidentally, I did not want food, only a drink.

When men went down the line, we did not always get them back. They were sometimes posted to other units, particularly drivers.

At the end of the next week, I was declared fit to travel so, shakily, I put on my uniform and out into the sunshine. I had above a mile to go, and I rested four times on the way. I was very shaky.

On my arrival at the Unit I went to report to the OC. He was pleased to see me, sorry I was not well, and then he plunged into the details of what had to be done. I enquired how many men were left – seventeen – so I asked him how all this work would be accomplished. 'Oh' said he quite haughtily, 'that is your job.' I never liked him after that, and it was nearly two months and one battle before we were back to being a Unit again.

In Palestine there were millions of fleas in some parts, particularly in the villages. One of our working parties near Gaza went into a water house (single story and built of stone).

The floor was covered with blankets belonging to the locals, and they were full of fleas – millions of them. Our men came out with their uniforms literally crawling, covered in the damned things. They undressed, shook their clothes and did everything they could to rid themselves of the pests but with little joy. They then returned to our lines and inevitably the fleas spread. A week later we had to move as the ground in our camp was so infested.

We bathed as often as we could, generally in a canvas bucket. In 1917, I went into the dugout occupied by one of the Corporals, an older man, as he was washing himself. I enquired if he was lousy and he said he had never had fleas or lice, this was incredible so I asked how he managed it. It was easy. Into his small amount of water in the bucket he put one teaspoon full of paraffin and rubbed himself down with a cloth. I looked at him standing there, naked, and his body shone. After that I started with it, gave it out on orders to the men and we were clear ever after. Surprising that the Army hadn't told us of this remedy from the outset, it would have prevented a lot of discomfort.

In April, we made another abortive attack on Gaza with a retirement and 9,500 casualties. Things were not going well with our Campaign. The Turks were a tremendous foe, as we had found out on Gallipoli and here they were dug in.

Defeat at Gaza

In the two battles for Gaza, which took place within three weeks of each other, the British were defeated. After the second battle, the British lines had moved forward but nowhere near as far as had been planned. The troops dug in to their forward positions just outside Gaza. It was April 1917.

During the second battle, a German aircraft landed. The pilot got out and blew up a section of the water pipeline before taking off again. This highlighted the fragility of the British supply lines.

The reason for the two defeats was considered to be due to the Allied attack being made at the strongest point of the Turkish defences and with troops advancing over open ground, in the face of heavy machine gun and artillery fire. The Allies had used tanks in the battle but this was the early days of tank warfare. Rather than grouping them together for an advance, they were used individually. As a result, each tank became an easy target for Turkish fire.

In both battles, the failure was attributed to poor planning and weak command. In London, confidence in General Murray evaporated and there was reluctance to send reinforcements until confidence in the campaign was restored. Murray was removed and a replacement was sought. The job was first offered to a South African general – Jan Smuts – but he turned it down and eventually, in June 1917, General Allenby was appointed. He had had success in France and was experienced in battle. During his first meeting with the prime minister, Lloyd George, Allenby was told to, 'take Jerusalem by Christmas'.

After their successful defence in the second battle for Gaza, the Turks began assembling a new army, bringing together their forces from other fronts including Salonika, the Caucasus and, after the Russian Revolution, from the Russian front in Anatolia. Additional German forces were also sent, and work started to build a new rail supply line from Turkish bases to the north and east into Gaza.

By this point the Turks were fighting on several fronts in the Middle East. They were facing British Forces advancing from Baghdad in the north east and from Sinai in the south, plus the Arab Revolt from the south and east.

My grandfather's next assignment would be with the Camel Corps in support of the Arab Revolt with Lawrence of Arabia.

The Arab Revolt and Lawrence of Arabia

Medina, Mecca and the Hejaz

The Arab Revolt began in 1916 in the Hejaz, the land around Mecca and Medina along the coast of the Red Sea.

In the early days of the war, the son of Sharif Hussein ibn Ali-el-Aun, Emir of Mecca, visited Cairo to find out how Britain would respond if his father's rule in the Hejaz was threatened by the regime in Constantinople. The Ottoman Sultan had appointed Sharif Hussein but when the Sultan was deposed in 1909, by the new regime in Constantinople, the Sharif's position was not touched, since he claimed ancestry descending from Mohammed. Nevertheless, the Sharif knew that the leaders in Constantinople, known as the 'Young Turks' were suspicious of him, and would depose him if they could.

The Sharif's son claimed that his father had the support of the other leading Arabs in the region, who would rally to his cause if he rose up against the Ottoman Empire. This was just what the chief of the Egyptian Army, Lord Kitchener, wanted to hear. He wanted to install a British supported man in Mecca, the Holy City of Islam, to show British support for the religion around the world. He also wanted to support an Arab uprising to throw the Turks out of the region to help defend the Suez Canal.

Kitchener sent a message to the Sharif suggesting that Britain would support a Caliphate at Mecca or Medina, hinting that, in due course, Hussein might become the Caliph of Islam. Not long after this, Kitchener was appointed as Secretary of State for War and left Egypt for London. Despite his departure, the British in Cairo started drawing up plans to support an Arab uprising in the Hejaz, and negotiations began with the Sharif over the terms for British support.

In June 1916, after much bargaining, and on hearing from his son, who had visited Constantinople, that there was a plan to depose him, Sharif Hussein finally agreed to rebel against the Turks. His forces took Mecca but not Medina.

As the situation in Gallipoli drew to a stalemate, the British began to seek other ways to undermine the Turks. They began to encourage the Sharif to expand his operations to push the Turks out of the region altogether. As part of this, in October 1916, the British high commissioner in Egypt, Sir Henry McMahon, wrote to the Sharif putting on paper the promise of British support for Arab independence after the war.

When the British leaders in India, and in the India Office in London, heard of this they were horrified. The idea of an independent Arab nation went against existing British policy, which was to divide and rule in the region. The view was also that McMahon had backed the wrong man and that they should have been supporting Ibn Saud – the man who would later overthrow Hussein and give his name to Saudi Arabia.

After receiving the letter from the British high commissioner, Sharif Hussein declared himself the King of the Arab Nation, not a title the British agreed with and not what they had intended. This caused difficulty. The British only ever referred to him as the King of the Hejaz. Money, in the form of gold sovereigns, together with guns and ammunition began to be shipped to the Sharif and his three sons. It is said that by November 1916, the British had armed over 20,000 Arab men in the region. At this point the Arab Revolt began in earnest.

With British reluctance to send Allied troops to the region, there was a recognition that something now needed to be done to organise Sharif's forces and to provide military advice and support. Captain T.E. Lawrence, later to be known as Lawrence of Arabia, was sent to the region in early October 1916 to review the situation after several failed attempts of Sharif's men to take the city of Medina. In particular, Lawrence was asked to advise on which of Sharif's sons could, and therefore should, lead the armed revolt. Lawrence jumped at the chance to go. He had been working in the Arab Bureau in Cairo until then, and had been somewhat bored. Also he had just lost his two younger brothers in the war in France. He wrote about how he felt it was wrong that he had an easy life in Cairo when they had given their lives in the fighting.

Lawrence had a first class honours degree in archaeology from Oxford, and had worked as an archaeologist in the Middle East before joining the army. He spoke Arabic and had learnt about the region of the Hejaz and the disposition of Turkish forces there from interviewing Turkish prisoners of war in Cairo as part of his military intelligence work. By all accounts, apart from a small group of close friends, he was not well liked by most of those around him. He was extremely intelligent and very self-confident, with an air of intellectual superiority.

His manner was described as more of an Oxford undergraduate than an army officer. Books written about his life describe how many dismissed him as an eccentric and said he didn't fit in. One British officer wrote that he thought Lawrence was a 'bumptious young ass' who deserved 'kicking and kicking hard'!

To meet the Sharif's sons, Lawrence had to ride into the interior of the Hejaz to where they were camped. This was dangerous. Christian infidels were not welcome in the region. Lawrence was given an Arab outfit to wear as a disguise and the journey took place at night. After the meeting, Lawrence decided that it was the Sharif's son called Feisal that had the best leadership qualities for the task at hand. The two got on well and, in the following months, Lawrence organised the delivery of arms and money, trained Feisal's fighters, gathered intelligence, liaised with Cairo and London and took part in the action.

Before the war, the Germans had helped the Turks to construct a railway line from Damascus to Medina, known as the Hejaz railway. This was being used by the Turks to supply their troops in the region, and was the obvious target for Arab attacks to prevent reinforcements from getting to Medina. Lawrence organised a campaign to blow up sections of the railway. The first success came on 17th February 1917 when, with support from a British Army explosives expert, a train on its way north from Medina was blown up.

As more raids took place to blow up sections of the railway, the Turks became more expert in finding the mines and in speedily repairing the line. The British engineers working with Lawrence realised that new tactics were needed. They began blowing up alternate rails and destroying curved sections, which were less easy to replace. They realised that if the explosion bent the rails then they were harder for the Turks to repair since it often meant replacing the whole section of track. To bend the rails the British devised 'tulip mines'. These involved placing a small amount of explosive under the sleepers, which blew the metal upwards at each end of the sleeper into a shape like a tulip. Whereas before they were using 40lbs of explosive for a single line of track, now they could render the same track useless with only 2lbs of explosive.

A major stopping point on the railway was at Ma'an. To the British, this looked like the point where Turkish supplies and troops would be brought for any attack on the Suez Canal. To defend against this, control of Akabah (now Aqaba) appeared vital, since it would give the British a base to ship troops and supplies. It was known that Akabah was well defended and was not somewhere that it would be advisable to land British troops for an attack. In July, Lawrence, with a group of Arab fighters, captured Akabah. This cut the Turkish supply lines into Sinai, helping the British forces in their advance into Palestine.

General Allenby met Lawrence in July 1917, and agreed to provide him with arms and support. My grandfather was sent as part of the signals support. British Forces sent to support Lawrence also included a troop of Egyptian Gunners. The history books describe how, after blowing up a train, the Arab fighters would descend to loot the train, almost oblivious to the gunfire around them. Tension arose when the Egyptian troops tried to stop the looting. Lawrence had to step in to mediate and calm things down.

History books report that throughout the campaign British troops complained about local Arab groups stealing from them. Apparently they were excellent at it. Soldiers slept with their boots on and with their rifles tied down. Various contraptions were set up as booby traps and alarms to catch the intruders but still they lost things. This built up hostilities between the British and the Arabs in the region.

As Feisal and Lawrence moved up country, the expectation in Constantinople of a British attack on Palestine meant that supplies and reinforcements could not continue to be sent to the Turks who were holding out in Medina. This meant that the Turks in Medina had fewer resources to pay local leaders to be part of their forces, so many began to leave and join Feisal and the Sharif.

Once Akabah had been captured in July 1917, Lawrence made plans for a campaign to support General Allenby's forces in the west of Palestine by attacking the Turks to the east of the River Jordan.

Throughout this time there were tensions with the French about the division of the Ottoman Empire after the war. The French were very suspicious of Lawrence and his intentions. He was keen to get to Damascus before the French to claim Syria for the Arab people but there were other political forces underway in London that later would put a different complexion on things.

With Lawrence of Arabia

As we pushed forward, we had to forgo the horses and take to camels. Then we became part of the Desert Mounted Corps and, later, Eastforce.

Camels are very peculiar animals. Usually, they are watered every other day and they drink about 17 gallons of water at a time, which takes them about 15 minutes. They can go for four or five days then, and if very short, could last seven days, although it is risky. The camel has such a habit of dying when he wants to. On trek all the camels would be apparently well and a halt at mid-day would occur. When moving off it would not be uncommon for one to have died completely out of the blue and for no apparent reason.

Camels smell and their riders get the benefit of it because they perspire first behind their ears – right in front of you as you sit there. They have to be oiled regularly, for they suffer from mange and lose their hair. I really didn't take to them. They are never friendly, either with man or their own kind. They always struck me as being the big bird that lost its wings. They carried their heads like a bird; if they had big wings they would look like an ostrich. But we needed them because with them we could carry our blankets and kit and three days rations, including water.

Once, on patrol, I had a large area to cover and had to bed down for the night. The camel knelt, and I hobbled him the usual way by tying the head rope around one front leg. As I took the saddle off he stood on three legs and started to walk away. It was a soft sand desert and impossible to run on it, but I knew if I didn't catch him I was done for. I struggled on as quickly as I could, threatening what I would do when I caught him as he used his three legs, but when I did catch him I tied the head rope round both his forelegs and that night I slept like a Bristolian – with one eye open. A near do.

Several battles were fought on the way, Roumani and others. When we reached a place appropriately called El Buggar (it had no inhabitants – just a map location, all soft desert sand and sun) a message came from HQ ordering us to take so many men and equipment to a map location south of the Dead Sea and report to Arab Command for duty. We were to work for Captain Lawrence – later known as Lawrence of Arabia.

I always took very careful compass bearings on the desert because there were no tracks, and we could easily be lost. I studied the map, worked out the distance and probable time for the journey.

We had camels and, as the pace of a camel on trek was two miles an hour on soft sand, we learned to estimate the time taken fairly accurately. As the sun always shone, albeit fiercely, we always knew the time of day and our direction. Nothing lived in this area except a few insects, and travel on a camel was boring. We took all the water with us, as we could not expect to find any.

In due course, we came across bands of Arabs who were surprised to see us and, for the first time, I saw a lot of English sovereigns, which they carried in their usual manner in bags slung round their necks hidden under their djellabas. They wanted to exchange the gold for Egyptian pound notes, currency they understood, but we were not paid enough to accumulate pounds so we couldn't oblige. Our Government paid the Arabs £20,000 a month to be on our side against their old enemies the Turks. They were armed with swords of all shapes and sizes, guns, both German and English carbines, and some old rifles. They had literally hundreds of camels and Arab ponies. A right mob, we thought.

At that time, the Arabs harassed the Turks, blowing up trains and stations at Mudawara and Ma'an on the Hejaz railway, which came from Aleppo to Medina. Their method of working was to find a suitable spot between hills that had culverts to allow water passage (if it rained). They placed explosives (tulips) under the rail tracks. Preparations for this were carefully done, and when completed the Arabs went over the hills, concealing their tracks by trailing blankets behind them. Then they waited.

Turkish soldiers guarded the trains. They had machine guns mounted on the roofs of the carriages, protected by sandbags. Quite a moving fort. As the train approached, the Arabs waited, concealed, for the explosion and then all hell was let loose. They were always numerically stronger but the Turks were stolid, careful soldiers who always defended themselves well and so a fight ensued, with the passengers getting the worst of it. No quarter was given and, as the Turks were overcome they were killed off. No prisoners were taken. The women were dragged over the sand, some by the hair, and were thrown across camels to be carried away. Then the train was pillaged and fights broke out over the spoils.

We had never seen anything like it. I had the greatest difficulty in restraining our boys from shooting some of them; they were so angered by the cruelty.

This incident biased our boys against the Arabs, and I was to be faced by objections and refusals to do various jobs for and with them. I reported this to one of our Officers attached to Lawrence's HQ and said we would like to be relieved of our tasks with them and return to our unit. I did not want it to turn into a shooting match, as it could well do.

Lawrence was just a little fellow, dressed as an Arab but with authority over them all. They were in the hands of the Sheikhs.

There was an incident that amused us. Whenever the British Army occupied a country, they always drilled the locals and armed them our way. In Egypt they formed a Mountain Battery with light guns and wheels and boxes of ammunition carried on camels. Considering that Egypt is mainly flat, this was surprising. The Egyptian Gunners were very smart, real parade ground soldiers, with orders in English. This Battery of four guns was attached to Lawrence's Arabs, and one day they had to go into action. Up they came, wheeled into place, each gun team the same distance apart. Camels knelt by order, the guns were assembled, camels to the rear and gunners knelt on one knee or stood to attention. The order was given to load but before they could fire, the Turkish guns fired two rounds, which burst near No.1 gun. Immediately, all the Egyptian soldiers ran away to their camels while we laughed. We knew the Egyptians by this time and it didn't surprise us.

When I think of the myths that were told about Lawrence and his Arabs I chuckled. They were, in fact, just bands of cut-throats without discipline. But for the money we gave them, they would have robbed us whenever they could. Lawrence and his Arabs were of little use to us. A lot was made of it for propaganda but the Indian Army were much more use and they had little praise or publicity.

Happily, our time with Lawrence was short as it did not match with our capacity, nor standard of work. They needed primitive communications, not the kind we supplied and my impression of them was that they were merely a nuisance to the Turks. We returned, much to our relief, and moved on towards Khan Yunis and Palestine to prepare for the attack on Gaza. Our horses returned and the camels went, another relief.

Not long after this, I was transferred to a newly formed Heavy Artillery Signal Unit. I had been promoted twice and I was transferred as Sergeant. I went down to Alexandria to train them. In 1917 I was offered a Commission but I declined. As you can tell, I wasn't impressed with that lot.

Third Battle for Gaza

After General Murray was relieved of his command, General Allenby went to Egypt and on to Palestine. This was soon after his appointment in June 1917. He visited the troops, and took time to speak to them and their commanding officers. He is described as someone who was prepared to listen and take advice from staff at all levels, and is said to have made a huge difference as soon as he arrived, quickly gaining the respect of the men. He appointed a new general staff and began to draw up plans for a new campaign. From this a list of requirements was sent to London for additional forces, guns, ammunition and aircraft.

Major works then started to improve the supply lines to the front including more radio stations to improve communications. The land around Gaza was reconnoitred.

Allenby's request for reinforcements was largely granted, and troops began arriving from mid-August. They came from all over the world including: East Africa, India, Aden, Hong Kong and Singapore.

Negotiations had already begun between the Allies about how to divide up the Ottoman Empire after the war. Italy had joined the Allies in May 1915, and wanted territory after the war in the Near East. The Italians decided that they needed to send troops to Palestine to be included in the negotiations after the war. The French had made it clear that they wanted to occupy the Lebanon and parts of Syria after the war and, since they were suspicious of the English intentions, they also sent troops.

A new mounted division was created. The Camel Corps was made up of volunteers from other units, selected for their adventurousness and willingness to try new things. In August, it became the Desert Mounted Corps.

More aircraft arrived and, by September, the British had gained the upper hand in the air.

During this time, new Turkish and German troops also began to arrive in Palestine but this took more time than the leaders in Constantinople had expected due to bottlenecks crossing the Bosphorous and crossing the Taurus Mountains. In addition, the gauge of the railway changed in Syria so the troops had to change trains to be able to move south. A shortage of rolling stock for the railways and a shortage of fuel for the trains also slowed down the movement of their troops to the frontline. Disagreements then began between the Turks and the Germans about the best strategy for holding the line in Palestine.

By late October, General Allenby was ready. His plans involved attacks all along the Turkish line from Gaza to Beersheba and beyond. Whilst the artillery was bombing Gaza, Beersheba was to be captured with its water supply intact. The Mounted Corps were then to push on to Tell esh- Sheria and Abu Hureyra. Once these were taken, they were to push north and west to surround the Turkish forces in Gaza. A deception was put in place to land troops on the beaches north of Gaza. Other deceptions were also employed, including the deliberate loss of an officer's notebook, which was found by the Turks before the battle.

The attack on Beersheba was a success following a famous Australian cavalry charge. The water supply was captured intact, as required. The plans thereafter worked, and the Turks began to retreat. Gaza was taken on 7th November 1917. The occupation of the town was organised, and supplies came ashore by boat but this was slower than anticipated and the pursuit of the Turks northwards was delayed. Nevertheless, by mid-November, Turkish lines had been split and the British forces reached the hills of Judea outside Jerusalem. Then there was plenty of fruit and wine for the Allied troops to enjoy – oranges were plentiful. In Jaffa the people returned to their homes and began to reopen the cafes and restaurants. Life for the Allied troops began to improve.

Battle for Beersheba, October-November, 1917

When the Heavy Artillery was put in Brigades, I was transferred from GHQ Signals as a Sergeant to train their Signals. In fact, six were transferred from different units, and I was the youngest of them. Soon, five were sent back to their units as unsuitable for training others, which left me the senior when the replacements came, and I was appointed Sergeant Major of the Company.

Norman, 1917

We trained in Alexandria and then went up the line for an attack on Beersheba.

Preparations for this were on a large scale. All previous attacks had been on the spot, and with little preparation due to the assumption that one British Sergeant and a Union Jack would frighten the enemy into submission. This concept had by now been exploded, and General Allenby came from France to take charge. He, of course, had only seen trench warfare but was a Cavalryman, and he prepared.

One day, we were running out some cables that had to cross the perimeter of an aerodrome and, as they were land lines, we had to bury them in a shallow trench to keep them out of the way of the planes. We had dug the trench and run out the lines preparatory to placing them below when an aeroplane was brought out preparing to take off. The plane came taxiing up to where we were working, then turned in the direction in which it had come and opened up to fly off. It came too near and, as the pilot opened up his engine, he fouled our cables and they, of course, held him back. So he stopped his engines and looked out of the cockpit. We told him what had happened and said we would clear up for him to go. He waited while one of our boys lifted the tail and another, underneath, tried to pull the wires clear. The pilot must have thought he had a signal, because all at once he opened up and moved forward. As he did so, his tail skid ran up the back of the chap underneath and, to our horror, started to drag him along the ground. His weight, of course, prevented the plane from moving quickly. We ran alongside, banging on the plane, so the pilot shut off and stopped.

Our boy was very shaken, the incident had taken the shirt off his back and the skin off his face and chest. He was quite white but how we pulled his leg afterwards about his flight hanging by his braces. They were Army issue and they didn't break! But we watched out after this.

Our Brigade was to open the attack in the Battle for Beersheba in an area that had only Cavalry Patrols, as it had previously been the right flank of our Army. It was flat country without cover, so the Army moved at night. We had our telephone lines laid and the guns (6-inch and 8-inch guns) moved into position. The first salvo was from the 6-inch batteries. The observers had not been over the ground before. Immediately in front was a viaduct on a railway line into Beersheba and, while I was looking, the first shells came over and hit the viaduct right in the centre. In no time, a train came to repair it and the guns fired again and hit the train. A magnificent effort. The battle developed and we were successful, moving up country. I never saw any better shooting during the war.

I was interested in Gaza because it was the home of Philistines, of whom there were said to be something like 60,000. That was where Samson and Delilah's story came from. I remember thinking at the time that there was nothing there that would lead me to believe that so many people had ever lived there. How would they irrigate the land when only one well existed? I had to arrange for the water in that one well to be chlorinated.

After the battle for Beersheba and Gaza, we moved forward to take Jerusalem. As we moved up country, we saw many things of interest and my previous readings as a boy proved of great value. I knew broadly the configuration of the country, its relationship with its neighbours and many of the stories, which had been told and retold by its religions and their adherents. Many of these I discounted as nonsense but I still preserved an open mind upon their application to people. In some way, I have always regarded a religion, any kind, as being a safety net for common people against the so-called state. It was something tangible yet intangible. It bound the people together in a common bond against authority, and gave them an opportunity to decide how they should be controlled. Its prophets tried to espouse a better life by eliminating the failings of man. It was always there to observe and comment, and kings, at times, used it to claim parity or precedence. These then were some of my thoughts as we entered the country.

The Sergeants or the Sergeant Majors increasingly ran the units. So it was no surprise when, in 1917, I was offered a Commission in the Air Force or the Infantry, to be taken up immediately. When I refused, they offered one in the Artillery. At the time, I was the Sergeant Major of the 1st Heavy Artillery Signals Co., which I helped to train upon its formation. I said I would take a Commission in the Signals but was ignored. My OC said I had the best job in the British Army and I would be foolish to go! Perhaps he was right. So I stayed with him but was pestered by the poor talent we had as Officers. Indeed, I grew to ignore some of them and ran the unit in my own way. In the last big battle when Jerusalem was captured, my OC was at a Headquarters 25 miles behind and kept in touch by telephone. They awarded him the Military Cross.

From this you will gather that I had contempt for many of those in command, but not all. Indeed, upon demobilization in 1919 my last OC came and spent a fortnight at my home and Colonel McLaren of Leeds offered me the facilities at their office canteen for a meal anytime that I was in Leeds (he was a Territorial).

Jerusalem: That Sacred Place

To the British, the capture of Jerusalem was now a specific war aim. The French and Italians wanted to stake a claim too. Discussions had been ongoing for some time between the Allies, and it was agreed that Italy would gain parts of Anatolia and Armenia would become Russian. Under what was known as the Sykes-Picot Agreement negotiated between Britain and France, France would gain the Lebanon and parts of Syria; Britain would take Mesopotamia and the oilfields; and Palestine would be subject to a joint Franco-British regime.

In a different agreement with the Arab leaders fighting with Lawrence, the British had cut across their agreements with France, agreeing instead for an Arab State in the region. Then, on 2nd November 1917, the British Foreign Secretary, Arthur Balfour, sent a letter to Baron Rothschild, a prominent Jewish leader in Britain, proposing that if the war was won then Palestine would become the designated home of all Jewish people.

The Balfour letter was the result of much diplomacy between the Allies, and it was debated in the Cabinet over several months. It had several aims: it was part of the deal to bring the Americans into the war, given their large Jewish population; it was designed to bring more Jewish money to the British war effort; and if it was agreed then the British would have to implement it, which would give Britain, not France, Palestine.

During the third battle for Gaza, the Bolsheviks seized power in Russia, and in November 1917 Trotsky circulated a plea to all sides for peace. By mid-December, he had agreed an armistice with Germany, and German troops were immediately redeployed to the Western Front in France. Allenby was asked to send troops to France. At the same time the War Cabinet worried about losing in Palestine. They knew that the Turks did not want to lose control of Jerusalem.

Given the proximity to Jerusalem, Allenby was given the go ahead to proceed to take the city but there was to be no fighting in or around Jerusalem, and it was stipulated that no holy places were to be damaged.

The Court of the Marquis of Northampton

We moved in from El Arish via Khan Yunis to Gaza, and then moved right to Beersheba, then up country via Ramallah to Jerusalem.

For some time our Unit of the Signals had been a Mobile Unit of General Headquarters Signals, helping other Signal Units to overcome their difficulties. We were specialists capable of undertaking any task, from ground cables to permanent line work, to organising Signal Offices and maintaining all the types of Army signal equipment. The men were all carefully selected for their knowledge and experience. Wherever we went, we were looked up to and respected. Our work was with all types of Units and formations, Brigades, Divisions, Corps, Balloon Sections, Cavalry and Infantry. Whenever our work ended, we returned to GHQ to be ready for the next assignment. It was interesting, sometimes tiring and often dangerous because we were frontline but we liked it because each man had a responsibility, making a good job of what he had to do, without much supervision. I was the Sergeant Major of the Unit at the time.

On this occasion, we were ordered to the 4th Cavalry Division to plan and build up their communications for the forthcoming attack.

As movement in the area was difficult in daylight because we were under observation by the enemy, we had to move at night. Having collected our stores and supplies, and studied our maps, we were ready to move off about 9pm to arrive at 4th Cavalry HQ before daylight the next morning. We had no difficulty in finding our way and arrived at 3:15am.

To our surprise, we were welcomed by the Sergeant Major of the 4th Cavalry Divisional Signals, Jack Sharp, who showed us where we could place our lines. I knew him as a Sergeant in the Territorials in the Northern Signals in Leeds before the war and so, for a few minutes, we yarned about it, talking about where we had been since.

When he left me, he said, 'See you at 6.'

I said, 'What for?'

'Our first parade is at 6.'

So I said, 'As our men have been on their way since 9pm, our first parade will be at 8am. And understand this – I am in charge of this Unit.'

So we had our parade at 8am.

The horses went off for water and were groomed on their return. The NCO in charge of the horse lines gave the order 'feed away' as soon as he saw that all the animals were satisfactorily groomed. The other men prepared the stores for the first job to be done. My OC had joined the Officers of the Divisional HQ in their mess. He was always content to leave the preparations to me.

Not long afterwards, the Orderly Officer came to look round our lines, accompanied by the Sergeant Major, so I stepped out to meet him. He complained that the order to 'feed away' was given before the horses had been groomed for an hour and that we had not observed their routine of drill for other units attached to them, to which I said that we were a unit of GHQ come to do a special job and were not attached to them for discipline. Obviously, he did not like that and said we must obey their orders. My reply was that if he had any orders for us he had better see my OC and arrange them accordingly.

Then, petulantly, he turned away and then back again to face me and said, 'Don't you salute an Officer when he leaves you?'

I said, 'Yes – as a rule.'

Then he went off with his Sergeant Major.

Later that day, when our working party returned, Sharp came across and said his OC, the Marquis of Northampton, and his court of Officers wished to see me in the Division Office at 6:30pm. So I asked him if it was intended to put me on a charge and what it was.

'Oh,' he said, 'I am not sure about that, but he was sore about your treatment.'

I also asked him if I should have an escort of equal rank. This was a usual thing, but he and I were the only ones of that rank, so it was a joke.

Well, in due course I attended the office. The Marquis sat at the head of the table with his Officers down each side and me standing at the bottom end. The Orderly Officer, who was about my age, told his story and he did it well. It sounded as if he had been badly treated when he retold it. One or two questions were asked and then I was invited to say something about it.

As my rank in a Unit needed knowledge of King's Rules and Regulations, I knew at that point that the 'court' could not order any punishment because the Rules as to 'charging a prisoner' had not been observed – i.e. no charge had been made in writing. If the rules were not followed, no further charge could be preferred which, in effect, left me free to say what I liked, within, of course, the other Army rules.

I told them the truth and suggested that perhaps we might not be with them long, depending upon the work to be done, and that we could manage our own discipline. We were proud of our Unit etc. and accustomed to being attached to other Units for food and water.

So it was 'talked out' and I was free to leave. As I went outside, I saw my OC and he said 'How did you get on?'

'Oh, they just talked about it – but I could have done with a "friend" and thought you might be there.'

He said, 'I was invited, but I told them that you could stick up for yourself without me. What are you going to do now?'

'I am parading our men to ask if they would prefer to move nearer the line, where our work will be, and leave this lot.' As a parting shot, I added, 'You could stay here with them in their mess and I will report each night on the work done that day.'

He did just that.

Our chaps nearly let me down because as we moved out next morning, their Units were on parade and someone in my Unit blew them a very loud raspberry.

The Capture of Jerusalem

The fight for Jerusalem took place during the first week of December 1917.

During the night of the 8th-9th December, the Turks silently withdrew through the city and headed north. The British knew nothing about it until the next morning when, cautiously, they approached the lines to find only a few snipers remaining. The Turks had taken all their munitions and withdrawn to regroup and fight again further north.

The Mayor of Jerusalem came out to surrender the keys to the city, and eventually found someone of sufficient rank. Major General Shea commanding the London Division accepted the keys and entered Jerusalem.

General Allenby made a ceremonial entrance to the city on 11th December 1917. He climbed out of his car and, diplomatically, walked into Jerusalem through a guard of honour made up of troops from each of the Allied countries.

After entering the city, Muslim troops from India were placed as guards on the Mosque of Omar alongside the traditional Muslim guardians.

Having captured Jerusalem, Allenby now had to turn his attention to pursuing and defeating the Turks.

Jerusalem: Life on the Mount of Olives

Jerusalem was a very small place with a wall round it and gates for entry. We lived in the Syrian orphanage that was then on the Mount of Olives.

When we first arrived, we had a conducted tour by one of our parsons, who told us not to laugh at the stories we heard from the guides at each of the holy sites, clearly there had been trouble during earlier visits. The city had very narrow streets with buildings of no account whatsoever. The Via Dolorosa was a hive of commercialism where even nuns sold postcards, olive wood ornaments and beads made in Czechoslovakia. This was not what we had expected.

The place of the Last Supper was akin to a small room over a dwelling. The Church of the Holy Sepulchre was, of course, the only Christian building, and surprisingly it was nothing to look at. It was occupied by Abyssinians on the roof; Coptics lower down, then Greek Orthodox and Roman Catholics. For one shilling a Catholic priest would lend you a candle to look at the Temple Curtain, which was 'rent in twain'. It was a piece of green marble with a crack in it. The tomb of Christ was in there, and we went and sat in it. It was brown marble with seats on each side. The one tawdry thing of note was a wax bust of the Virgin Mary on the altar, decorated with rings on every finger, bracelets, tiaras and necklaces of every kind. Catholics from all over the world had taken or sent them. We were told that the King of Spain gave thousands of pounds each year just to be called, 'His Most Catholic Majesty'. No doubt he would put it about that God had called him to that office.

The only other building of note was the Mosque of Omar. In the centre of that was a rock, considered by the Ancients to be the actual centre of the earth and upon which the Ark of the Covenant rested, and it was also supposed to be the spot where Abraham sacrificed Isaac. Underneath was a hole where Mohammed prayed and, according to the story, he prayed so fervently one day that he actually knocked a large piece off with his head.

We were in the town some weeks. The population I recall was mainly Arab with only a few Jews.

From Jerusalem we went down to Jericho and on to Amman in Jordan, then back to the Jordan Valley and the Dead Sea. We went to Jericho then forward to Nablus, down to the plain of Esdraelon and forward again to Haifa, taking in the coastal places such as Acre and Sidon.

In the final battle we were in Haifa.

From Jerusalem

The Turks had retreated north up the Nablus Road and eastwards to the River Jordan, keeping up a fierce fight with regular attacks on Allied forces.

Allenby contemplated staying in Jerusalem but realised that he needed a stronger frontline, which could only be achieved by pushing on to join up with the British forces advancing from Baghdad. He was under pressure to send troops to France, which meant that his forces were being diminished. This in turn made the next phase of the campaign more difficult. With fewer troops, he took time to reinforce his supply lines before moving on from Jerusalem.

In February 1918, British forces pushed eastwards, capturing the land to the Jordan Valley and Jericho. In March, the line to the west of Jerusalem began to advance northwards towards Nablus.

At the end of March, British and Arab forces joined in a battle with the Turks and Germans over several days but failed to take Amman. The second battle for Amman took place in September 1918, and was a success for the Allies, with Turkish forces retreating. Following this victory, the British continued to pursue the Turks northwards and eventually captured Damascus on 1st October.

On the 30th October 1918, the Turks sued for peace. The First World War in the Middle East was over.

To Haifa via Armageddon, 1918

The attack on the Nablus Road had been successful (19th-25th September 1918). The Turks retreated rapidly, and we were ordered to proceed to Haifa. Our way from Jerusalem was down the road through the Judean Hills to the plain called Armageddon, and thence northward, level with the coast. It was easier going once we left the hills and at Latrun, in the foothills, we stayed in a monastery habited by Trappist monks. They did not speak to anyone, and as we used their cells for sleeping and their cookers and fires for preparing food, it seemed strange to us that they were always silent but we saw this as their meditation. We knew they were up early in the mornings and, after food and prayers, went out to work in the vineyards and they made very good wine, a Tokay, supposed to be as good as anything in the world.

The stay in the monastery was really a strange interlude. Fortunately, our boys were always well conducted, and we impressed upon them that they must treat the monks with respect – and not drink too much wine. We paid for the bottles we drank, at that time two shillings each. When we left, the monks turned out and waved to us, but did not speak. We did, and thanked them heartily for their forbearance. When we arrived, we thought that they were probably Italian and did not understand English and that was why they did not speak, so it passed over but when we were leaving they made it clear, by signs, that they knew what we were saying.

It was an experience, but not one that appealed to our boys. The idea of living with others and saying nothing just could not be borne!

We travelled north up the plain, level with the coast, passing through several Jewish settlements on the way and buying wine at each. The people were glad to see us as they were tired of the Ottoman administration, or lack of it. We drank wine in our mugs, and somehow we were overcome by it at times. When we stopped for the night and made a camp we had to make a rule that the Night Guards should not have any wine because they fell asleep, allowing the locals to raid the camp and steal our clothing and equipment before vanishing into the shadows. They would take with them all kinds of things, for they had little, and everything of ours had a real value to them. Poverty creates these conditions.

Eventually, we arrived in Haifa, a seaside town, not much of a place, with a ridge of land running down to it from the hills inland – the end of the ridge being Mount Carmel. The streets were very narrow, and the houses had steps outside the doors. When our ammunition lorries went up the street, they pressed each of the house steps into the ground. We thought it a joke, but the natives did not, and the steps were replaced shortly afterwards. In Haifa we met our first Jewish Battalion coming ashore from a troop transport. They needed transport too for we had never seen so much for one unit before. We were asked to provide lorries. After a day or two, our lads grew tired of it and it was surprising how many vehicles ran off the road or broke down in the ensuing fortnight.

We were happy here because we could bathe in the sea and we went fishing. Our lines were not much use, so we took a boat and, offshore, dropped a Mills bomb in the water. The explosion brought dozens of fish to the surface, all stunned, and we just paddled round and collected them. Some came round quickly and swam away before we could collect them but it was a useful addition to our diet. It did not last long, however, as High Command heard of it and forbade it. I do not know on what grounds but it may have been the local fishermen protesting at their catch being caught by us.

From our journey through Palestine we had a complete picture of all that we had been taught in our early years at school, and we strove to compare that with what we saw. That was important – what we saw. We found extreme poverty everywhere. Both Arabs and Jews existed on very little. In the country districts there were vines on the terraced hills and olive trees. On the land that could be cultivated, a small attempt had been made at ploughing with a camel or donkey. There were some palm trees near Gaza at Deir el Belah. In all, there was an aura of poverty and neglect everywhere. Perhaps the oranges grown around Lydda were the bright spot but they had to be carried away on the backs of camels.

Looking at the villages and the Jews and Arabs living in Palestine, their poverty and absence of decent homes and buildings, made me wonder why we had been taught that it was such a wonderful land when, in fact, it was so barren and poverty-stricken. The Lord God certainly had not improved it, nor the conditions of the people. I thought of the hymns we sang in church and at Sunday school – *There is a Green Hill Far Away* – we could not find one there!

Nablus, Haifa, Jericho and Samaria, were all nothing to look at. Jaffa was a small port, with probably more Jews than Arabs living there. There was some wild corn grown south of Gaza, and the Bedouin came each year to take it when ripe.

Altogether, Palestine was a disappointing place, not worth fighting for. Indeed, I wondered why our government even thought of sending troops there. I am sorry to say it, but the Campaign there achieved nothing, indeed it probably caused more trouble in the end. The kudos of capturing the holy places from the Turks does not bring comfort to the wives and mothers of those who gave their lives for democracy or those boys who wasted some of their young years in hardship and danger.

The War on the Western Front, 1918

The Western Front

After the Russians exit from the war in late 1917, German forces on the Eastern Front were redeployed to the west to France and Belgium. At this time, the Allies realised the need to coordinate their efforts along the Western Front, having been fighting largely as independent forces up until then with the British occupying the northern section of the line. The need for coordination was increased by the arrival of large numbers of American soldiers – over 250,000 every month. The Frenchman, General Ferdinand Foch, was appointed to oversee and coordinate the efforts of the British, French, Italian and American forces.

The Americans had entered the war in 1917 but did not possess a large standing army. They had never fought overseas, and had no experience of trench warfare. Their men were new recruits who needed training, equipping and transforming into a fighting force. This took well over a year. To begin with, the British and French Generals argued that American troops should be integrated into their armies, as the Australian and Canadian forces had been, but the American General Pershing held firm and, by July 1918, the First US Army had been formed and was in place defending a stretch of the Western Front around Verdun.

With the arrival of troops from the east, the Germans launched a major offensive in March 1918, known as the Spring Offensive. They made huge territorial gains, but failed to break through the Allied lines. The Allies needed reinforcements and, in Palestine, General Allenby was asked to release as many of his experienced forces as possible; gradually more were sent.

The German offensive continued over the following months. Then, on 15th July, they made one last major attempt to break through and reach the city of Rheims.

The July offensive took place along a 65-mile front using 42 German Divisions but the Allies were ready and waiting. Intelligence had warned them of the impending attack, and new defensive tactics were brought into play. Earlier in the war, German offensives had been repelled with a solid line of troops in the frontline trenches but this meant huge losses. The Allies realised that it was more effective to place the bulk of their forces behind the frontline at a distance that caught the Germans when they were tired and over-extended – a tactic known as the 'mouse trap'. This worked, and, by the 17th July, any hopes the Germans had of reaching Rheims were gone. Then the Allies struck back, seizing the initiative away from the Germans.

By 1918 Allied offensive tactics had changed too. The Allies had air power over the Germans, led by the French who had the world's largest air force. Tanks were now central to operations and surprise was the order of the day. Gone were the huge barrages of artillery announcing that troops were about to come over the top. This time there was an enormous build up of tanks, guns and troops behind the lines, quietly and well hidden with planes drowning out any noise and keeping the German air force at bay to stop them seeing what was happening.

At dawn on 17th July, French, American and Italian forces sprung a surprise counterattack on the Marne Front. German high command was stunned, and a retreat on this part of the Front began on 20th July. For the first time in months, the Allies had the upper hand.

By 1918, the British naval blockade was having an immense effect in Germany and Austria-Hungary. All possible food supplies to the Central Powers had been stopped. Prices began to rise; people in Germany, Austria and Hungary began to starve. Feeding the troops became more and more difficult. During the Spring Offensive, reports were received of German troops stopping to eat the copious food supplies in the Allied trenches and having to be forced to move on by their commanding officers.

Malnourishment also contributed to the spread of infections. In June and July, flu spread through the German Army with over half a million men being taken ill. The huge casualties combined with the numbers of malnourished and sick led some senior officers to argue for a retreat to a line that could easily be defended but those in the German high command would not listen.

Word of the retreat on the Marne was received in letters at home. With the people starving, and with morale sinking, civil unrest began in Berlin and in other cities. After the overthrow of the Tsar in Russia, many in Germany now supported a revolution and called for the overthrow of the Kaiser and the German high command.

A further surprise attack at Amiens in August saw the Allies advance over 6 miles into German-held territory. Reports came in to German high command of huge numbers of their troops surrendering – many in need of food – and others retreating and shouting out to the men coming to reinforce the lines that they were prolonging the war. There was also a dawning realisation that they did not just have to defeat the British and the French, now there were thousands of American troops ready to fight.

On 13th August, General Hindenburg, commander in chief of German forces held a meeting in his headquarters in the town of Spa in Belgium about what to do next. The conclusion was that victory was out of sight and peace was needed. The following day, after a meeting with the Kaiser, a tentative approach was made to the Allies. However, as the fighting went on, morale in the high command began to swing. At times there was optimism with senior officers thinking there was no need for peace talks, especially if the heavily fortified Hindenburg Line could be defended.

In September, my grandfather's heavy artillery section was dispatched from Palestine and sent to Albert in France. The same month, the British Forces began a fierce attack towards Cambrai and St Quentin – moving forward from their bases in Amiens and Albert. This was one of the toughest sectors of the German defence but on the 29th September, supported by the heavy artillery, Canadian forces broke through.

Throughout September, the Allies kept up their surprise attacks all along the Western Front but they could not advance fast enough. At certain points they had to stop to allow communications to be established, for heavy artillery to be moved forward and for supplies to be organised. All this gave the Germans time to retreat to more defensible positions, and soon they occupied the strong defensive positions along the Hindenburg Line. The Allies advance then slowed.

The Allies had also made progress in Salonika. In Bulgaria, food shortages had also led to civil unrest and strikes. Disobedience began to spread through the Army. The Allies attacked north of Salonika and the Bulgarian Front collapsed – the Army simply went home. Around the same time, the Turks also began peace talks and Austria-Hungary indicated they were on the verge of suing for peace too.

With the failure of their partners in the war, the German high command now realised that an armistice was needed, especially before the Allies reached German soil. Their hope was that the Allies would want peace to such an extent that they would allow the German Army to retreat intact to within the German borders.

On 3rd October 1918, a telegram was sent from the German Chancellor, Prince Max, via the Swiss Government to the American President, Woodrow Wilson, arriving on 6th October. In it was acceptance of President Wilson's fourteen points for peace set out in his speech to Congress in January 1918 and a request for peace negotiations to begin. The next day a similar letter arrived from the Austro-Hungarians.

President Wilson's fourteen points for peace were:

1. Open covenants of peace, openly arrived at
2. Freedom of the seas
3. The removal so far as possible of all economic barriers
4. The reduction of national armaments to the lowest point consistent with domestic safety
5. Impartial adjustment of all colonial claims
6. The evacuation of all Russian territory
7. The evacuation and restoration of Belgium
8. The liberation of France and return to her of Alsace and Lorraine
9. Readjustment of the frontiers of Italy to conform to clearly recognisable lines of nationality
10. The peoples of Austria-Hungary should be accorded the freest opportunity of autonomous development
11. Evacuation of occupation forces from Romania, Serbia and Montenegro; Serbia should be accorded free and secure access to the sea
12. Autonomous development for the non-Turkish peoples of the Ottoman Empire; free passage of the Dardanelles to the ships and commerce of all nations

13. An independent Poland to be established, with free and secure access to the sea

14. A general association of nations to be formed to guarantee to its members political independence and territorial integrity (the genesis of the League of Nations)

The request for an armistice was reported in the papers on the 6th October 1918, two days after the Allies had broken through the Hindenburg Line. Nevertheless, some German troops continued to put up a stern defence and fighting continued. Cambrai fell on 9th October, and the retreating German soldiers began a scorched earth policy, destroying and burning everything in sight. Booby traps were set up to catch the advancing forces including poisoned food. Anything that the soldiers might touch unawares was linked to explosives such as the steps on stairs. Even playing a piano could be deadly.

During this time, German submarines continued to torpedo ships in the Atlantic, including passenger liners and many Allied soldiers, sailors and politicians (especially the French) wanted to press on until the German Army surrendered in Berlin. There were also disagreements and issues between the Allies – the French did not want the Americans dictating the terms of the peace and the British did not agree with Wilson's second point and were determined to keep control of the seas. The peace was not going to be easy to achieve.

In his reply to the German Chancellor, President Wilson demanded an immediate halt to submarine attacks and the policy of scorched earth and destruction as the German forces retreated, saying that fighting would not stop until these came to an end.

This was contested but eventually agreed by the Germans on 21st October.

The next point was that the Allies were unwilling to allow the Kaiser and the German high command to remain in charge of the army when there was no oversight of their actions by the German people through Parliament. Allowing their army to retreat to within the German borders without a change in the leadership or the power of control over the army was unacceptable, especially to the French who feared another war. So, in the next correspondence, President Wilson demanded the abdication of the Kaiser, saying that if the Allies had to deal with the current military leaders and not the real rulers of Germany – the people through the Parliament – then the demand was for Germany to surrender.

The German high command were furious. They began making plans to send more troops to the front, planning a new line to retreat behind and defend. But, as the Allies continued to advance, it was clear that the writing was on the wall. By the end of October, both Hindenburg and his deputy Ludendorff had resigned. The Kaiser refused to accept Hindenburg's resignation but it was not long after, on the 4th November 1918, that the German Chancellor told the Kaiser that his abdication was necessary to prevent a revolution and civil war.

On the 9th November 1918, after speaking to his new high command on their willingness to fight on, the Kaiser abdicated and departed for exile in the Netherlands.

To France and the Western Front, 1918

When it was apparent that the Palestine Campaign was won and our troops were as far as Haifa, there was talk of withdrawing one Brigade from each Division, substituting an Indian Brigade for them.

The Italian Army was in difficulty, having collapsed at Caporetto, and the first troops to leave went there. With them went the 60th Brigade of Heavy Artillery. Then our Brigade was ordered to France and, in due course, we moved down to Port Said for embarkation. We had a very pleasant voyage through the Mediterranean, where we were able to relax on board and enjoy the sun and the scenery. We sailed past Cyprus, Crete, Sicily and Corsica before approaching Marseilles. It was marvellous seeing those islands that we had read about, and we leaned over the rails and waved at the local fishermen as we passed.

Marseilles was bustling and busy with supplies being landed from all over the world. I led Timbuc down the gangway and bought him some apples. We enjoyed some French wine and I tried to speak to the locals but my Arabic was much better than my French by then.

We went from the port through the narrow streets to a camp just outside the town where we were kitted out with warm clothing and we said goodbye to our drill tunics and shorts. Northern France was going to be very different to the heat of the desert. We had heard some stories of the misery in the trenches from lads who had joined us in Egypt, and so it was with some trepidation that, after two or three days, we boarded the train for the north.

We travelled through France by way of the Rhône Valley, a lovely journey for a holiday I thought – but this was no holiday. Eventually we arrived at Amiens, and then moved near Albert where the Batteries took up their positions.

Things were in a state of confusion because the Germans had broken through the lines of the Eighth Army, which had retired in face of the strong attack. Every available man had been taken to stem the advance but, apparently, the German soldiers who had captured NAAFI canteens and stores of food had hesitated to do some looting and our troops managed to reform to resist them.

The guns had been moving up to their prepared positions for some weeks, and ammunition of all types was brought by horse wagons, lorries and a Decauville light railway – a narrow gauge railway capable of being moved easily – to the lines every day until the dugouts were full to overflowing. This was something we had not seen before. In the early days, we had nothing much but as the heavy Artillery developed, things gradually improved. The 18-pounder Field Artillery had five guns per Battery, the 4.5 Howitzers were developed during the war, and so were the 6-inch, 8-inch and 10-inch howitzers, all very good guns. The 6-inch guns were used for barrage, the cover behind which the

Infantry advanced in a battle, and the other Howitzers were for counter Battery and long range support.

Before an attack started, there was always a lot of preliminary work, putting enemy batteries out of action, all targets previously assembled in association with the Flying Corps and Sound Rangers who observed enemy guns. On this occasion, the gun pits, 12 feet deep, had all been prepared, with the result that the guns could calibrate as soon as they were ready.

We put out our lines of communications, which were rather more temporary than usual, and in a reasonable time ammunition stores were accumulated and firing began.

It was obvious that a very large attack was being prepared after the Germans nearly broke through. We were supporting an Irish Division. The night before our attack started, a squadron of Bombers, Handley Page, poured a ton of bombs upon the German Signals Headquarters, and then firing began in earnest. Not a single German plane came over our lines and got back because they were chased by numbers of our aeroplanes and driven inland.

We were given details of the batteries in front of us, 4.5 Howitzers, 18-pounder Field Guns, in all, on a five-mile front, 2,500 guns of various calibre. On the morning of the commencement of the battle, they all went off together. We were told later that the noise could be heard in England. This continued day and night for seven days, and the ammunition came up so well that the gun pits were always full. Actually, when the attack began, it was as a bombardment day and night for four days, with all kinds of shells from gas to high explosives, and this time it was concentrated on the frontline trenches, supports and enemy Battery positions.

As each Battery came into position on our part of the front, the guns calibrated on a German tank on a ridge immediately before us, which had been disabled in an earlier battle. It was arranged that each heavy Battery would land one round every twenty minutes on the tank, which the enemy used as an observation post, and with the number of heavy guns on the five miles of our part of the front a big shell would arrive every second.

On the eighth day, the Infantry moved forward over the shell-packed ground behind the barrage but the Germans had moved a fresh Division forward to resist. As the trenches had been bombarded so heavily, they had almost disappeared and were little more than holes in the ground, so our men were brought back and the guns ordered to recommence their firing. Our guns gave them another three days and nights, with gas shells included. The new enemy Division was caught. Ammunition supply was excellent and there were, in fact, more shells in the pits than when the action started.

After three days our Infantry went forward and captured the German lines. I had made arrangements for one of our cable wagons to move up to one of the forward observation posts and then to move forward with the advancing troops. At the end of that day we were 6 miles forward, passing all the debris and noticing the accuracy of our guns on the enemy positions. Our shells had been remarkably accurate. The Germans had taken some of their guns but left all their other things lying around. I warned the men not to pick up souvenirs because of booby traps, and it was as well that I did because there were several instances of men entering dugouts and bombs exploding.

That night, as the road ran between two low hills, the Germans stood to resist our advance and our 6-inch Howitzers were brought forward under machine gun fire to blast them off their positions firing with open sights, something we hadn't seen before. By morning, the guns reported that they had no targets. We had captured 350 guns of various calibres and all other stores. We moved on until we were 18 miles forward. Our link with Corps HQ was maintained, and our Infantry were in the enemy Divisional HQ.

During our advance, our planes had an enormous advantage, not a German plane crossed our lines and got back again for a whole month. If one tried, it was a common sight to see as many as a dozen or so chasing him to our rear, so that he could not get back home again. The night before the attack started, 21 Handley Page bombers dropped a ton of bombs each on the German's main Signal Headquarters thereby depriving them of their communications. Every one of us knew that this time it would be different.

The lorries with food and ammunition continued arriving for the next four days. Our boys showed them where to park.

We knew the enemy was in retreat, and that we had the upper hand. So we waited for the end, with a sense of satisfaction.

We moved up about thirty miles and then stopped. The next thing we knew was that the Germans had asked for an armistice, and that it had been granted with effect from 11am on 11th November 1918.

Then everything became quiet. No shells bursting.

It seemed unreal not to have the sound of guns by day and night.

We celebrated with a few drinks and some singing. It wasn't such a lively affair because I think many of us didn't believe it would last. Indeed, some of our men thought the Germans would start shelling us again in the morning. Nevertheless we took time to remember our comrades who had fallen, and had a drink or two for them. We slept well that night for the first time for several weeks.

Now I dreamt of home after four and a half years away but it was not until July of the following year that I was demobilised and came home.

In the months after the Armistice, we went on a mission to salvage and retrieve some of the costly items expended in our communications set up. We picked up about £2,000[24] of telephone wire each week from the cable trenches. We had to take care to avoid any unexploded munitions. It took time for the dead to be collected and buried, and although we were relieved the war had ended we had a constant reminder of the horrors all around us.

How I longed to go home.

---

[24] £100,000 today.

The End of the War

The German Armistice Commission arrived by train to the station at Rethondes in the forest of Compiègne, France, on 8th November, and peace negotiations began in earnest the next day.

The fighting continued right up until the signing of the Armistice on the 11th November at 11am. The war was over.

All Over But We Can't Leave, 1919

Eventually, in June 1919, I was told I was to be demobilised. We set off on the train north from Amiens, and eventually arrived in Boulogne. I was on my way home.

It was quite a difficult time, saying goodbye to my comrades. We had been together through thick and thin, and had seen each other safely through, so parting was hard. We shook hands and said our farewells.

A day or two before embarking on the returning ship, we were sent to Wimereux on the hill above Boulogne where there was a decontamination unit, run by German prisoners. As the Company Sergeant Major I had, on all occasions, to be smartly dressed, washed, shaved and 'on parade'. So, naturally, my clothing was spotless and my underclothing too.

The arrangement at the centre was to walk in single file down a long counter, handing in along the way all our pieces of equipment, then our uniforms in order (jacket, cap, trousers, then underclothes). We then had to walk along a corridor at the end of which sat a doctor who examined us for signs of venereal disease. Then we went under showers, collected a towel and proceeded up the other side where underclothes and, finally, a uniform which had been fumigated were handed out.

The clothes I had handed in were first class, but in return I was given one sock which was ankle length and the other up to my knee, a shirt that had been taken from a casualty or a dead man, all discoloured, and a pair of trousers with one leg shorter than the other. This was demeaning. When I protested the Officer said it didn't matter as we should be home soon, discharged, and anyway that was all they had. I had not been home for nearly five years and I didn't want my mother to see me in that get up.

We left Boulogne for Dover the next day but I felt disgraced. To think that was all the thanks we got for all those years of service to our country. I did my best to tidy myself up.

When I arrived in Wakefield my mother and sisters were waiting for me. I remember my mother's embrace, just as when I had left for war five years earlier. We all cried. What a relief it was to be home. I can't adequately describe my feelings at that time – the pain and sadness of loss mixed with the joy and happiness of coming home. I never told my mother and sisters about the war, and somehow they knew not to ask. Annie's young man had been killed in 1915.

We had plenty of visitors in the following weeks, who were all there to welcome me home. Many had lost sons and brothers in the war but were pleased for our family that I had returned. I had been injured but not seriously. I had a lump of shrapnel lodged in my back that stayed there for many years until it was taken out by a surgeon during an operation I was having for something else. I also had a tattoo of the Sphinx on my arm that I was embarrassed about – the result of a good night out in Cairo. I wore long sleeves thereafter.

When I was in Palestine, I had heard that my great pal 'Wilkie' Wilkinson had been killed. I went back to my old unit to enquire.

I was told he took a risk that they thought foolhardy, 'If you had been here Norman he wouldn't have done it.'

Poor Wilkie; I was sad. He was such a brave, likeable boy: flaxen hair always out of place, fair skinned, slim. That was 1917. I should have gone to see his sisters when I got home, there were five of them and they lived in Leeds, but I just couldn't face it – what would I say? How would they react given that I had survived? I doubted that I would have held together so I duffed it.

The last I heard of my other pal, Albert Jones, was that he was in Wakefield in a mental hospital and died there. He was truly the bravest of the three of us. Again I should have visited but couldn't. The pain was too great.

Things had changed at home while I had been away. Mother and my sisters Annie and Winnie had moved, and were now living in Wakefield. My sisters were both teaching in the county. My elder sister, Annie, was headmistress of a senior girls' school in Moorthorpe near Doncaster. I had to get used to life in a new town, and make new friends. I needed a job too. I talked to the principal of the firm in Leeds where I had worked before the war. He was quite prepared to take me back on the terms of my original agreement but, as I should have the cost of travel from Wakefield, I could not manage on 5 shillings a week,[25] so I began looking for another post.

I was soon successful in my search and started work in August 1919, in the property and deeds department of the West Riding County Council. Times were exceedingly difficult then, and really I was fortunate, more fortunate in fact that our

---

[25]   £2.25 today.

neighbours who, almost without exception, were on short time or out of work.

I asked myself was this what we had been fighting for? I could see why it had taken so long to bring the boys home after the war was over. There was no work. Many were on the scrap heap. I despised the politicians who had taken us into war and who were now making life so hard for the men that had served their country. I often thought of leaving the country to make a new life elsewhere. I had worked with the Australians and liked their attitude, and a life in Australia looked attractive, but could I leave my mother and sisters once again?

The man who returned

That winter I entered for a course at the technical school to brush up my business knowledge. It was difficult because our work in the office was behind due to staff going away to war, and we were expected to work overtime in order to bring it up to date. No payment was made. That wasn't a part of our agreement, and I did over 400 hours for nothing apart from one and sixpence tea allowance at a local café. We used to put the date under the paper holding the buns in the cafe to see how often they reappeared. It was a happy department, with so many returned ex-service men that discipline was largely self-imposed. We had an excellent chief, a barrister, who lost his only son in the war. He was one of nature's gentlemen but heartbroken.

My salary was on a pre-war rating plus a cost of living bonus (which was actually more than my salary) and before long we had the government saying that salaries and wages were too high, we were not competitive in the world and we should have to take less because the country was destitute. This, of course, led them to reducing miners' wages and increasing their hours, and there was an immediate strike with the usual cries of party politics in favour or otherwise. Gradually, I realised that those who 'had' did not wish those who 'had not' to climb up to their level.

In 1920, I was asked if I would become the departmental representative to serve on the Executive Committee of the West Riding County Staff Association. This association had been in operation for many years, and represented the staff in negotiations with the county council. I accepted, and thus began my work in the trades union movement with the National Association of Local Government Officers (NALGO).

At that time I also became a member of The Benevolent Society in order to do what I could to help the poor and those who needed temporary assistance because of unforeseen circumstances. Benevolent work became part of my life, and when I joined the Electricity Board, I began their Benevolent Society – it eventually became a national scheme, with over 10,000 members.

Despite my continuing sadness about the futility of the war and the conditions for the men who returned, life had to go on, and in 1920 I started to have singing lessons and competed at Pontefract and other nearby towns in their competitions and festivals. In 1921, I was introduced to a wonderful young lady called Clara. We courted and married in the beginning of 1926. We would have married earlier but it was impossible to obtain a house in Wakefield or anywhere near. They simply were not being built. Indeed, council houses were being built on such a small scale that they were almost unobtainable by families, who were instead forced to live in crowded conditions with their 'in-laws'. In any case, we decided that we wanted to buy one and it was not until 1925 that we were successful.

Norman's wife, Clara

In 1926, the year of our marriage, my cost of living bonus was reduced each month until in December it was £92 lower than in the January of that year[26]. No wonder feelings ran high and the number of unemployed rose to 1.5 million. We went along to the General Strike of 1926. This, to me, was the revolution that I always foresaw. It was bound to come at some time after the forces returned, especially with the poor rewards we received for the service and sacrifices made. We felt we had been deceived and the trades unions were the only means of expressing our feelings. The *May Report*, the *Ray Report*, the *Geddes Axe*, all followed the pattern of the government trying to reduce wages and the cost of living bonuses.

Gradually, over time, I managed to put the war years behind me. On a happy note, in 1927, our son, Peter Marshall, was born,

---

[26] A pay cut of around £4,900 today.

and in 1931 our daughter, Dorothy Mary[27], arrived. We became a family. My love for Clara and her love for me grew stronger over the years, and we were very happy. We were so very proud of our children, and they gave us hope for a more prosperous and peaceful future.

Our children, Dorothy and Peter

Family holiday in Bridlington — from left, Peter, Mother, Clara, Annie, Winnie and Dorothy in front

---

27 Susan's mother.

A Heart-Breaking Farewell to my Best Friend, Timbuc

Many times over the years, my grandchildren have asked me why I was crying, and I told them it was about my best friend, Timbuc. Just writing about him now brings tears to my eyes.

During the war years, I rode most days, and looked after horses, both day and night. They were warm to sleep against. I also taught new recruits how to ride. Often, when out on reconnaissance, we would come across enemy Cavalry and sometimes had to run for it, especially when there were four of us and twenty of them. Our horses were better and faster, especially Timbuc.

So I had him until my war ended in 1919, and the day was fixed for me to go home. We had had many adventures together. He had carried me everywhere. We had slept together at night. His speed got me out of trouble on many occasions. He was always ready for a gallop. We had been together for almost five years.

Men began to be demobilised, and the burden of looking after horses became greater. There weren't enough men to look after the horses, and we had less and less use for them. At that time we were six horses over strength (including Timbuc) so I ordered the NCO in charge of the horse lines to part with five.

One Artillery Captain took the two horses he wanted, and two others, strong draught animals, were given to the Labour Corps.

The question of what to do about Timbuc was in my mind. I felt that I could not leave him to an unknown fate. I had seen what was happening to the other horses that were no longer needed. Some were being taken and shot for horsemeat, others were being shipped off but no one knew where to or what for. With demobilisation, there were thousands of horses to be disposed of and I knew that Timbuc would be just one amongst them all if I left him with no one to look out for him.

We were very wrong to subject intelligent animals to such cruelty in the war. Man really stands condemned.

Timbuc and I understood one another, and we knew, almost instinctively, what one another would do. It was a happy relationship. One can get very attached to a good horse. I suppose, in total, I must have spent many hours with an arm round his neck talking to him. He would nod his head in agreement.

I would have liked to 'buy him out', and thought about this for many nights. How would I pay for this? I had no money to speak of. How would I care for him at home? I hadn't anywhere to keep him and, of course, no work for him and no income to pay for his keep. I did not want him to fall into any other hands abroad, and feared for his future if I left him. I had many sleepless nights. This was one of the most difficult decisions of my life. I spoke to the Farrier.

Having been with the horses for four years, the Farrier knew them well and he knew our feelings too. After reflection, he said, 'Why not shoot him?'

283

I stood there speechless for some time.

'You will know what happened to him and it will be done quickly and kindly – he won't suffer you know.'

We had shot many horses during the war to end their suffering when they were injured in the fighting. Oh dear, was he right?

I turned away and walked into the wood nearby and cried until I could cry no more. I had seen men die, my comrades dead or injured and I hadn't cried like this. This would be like shooting my brother but I couldn't leave him to an unknown fate either.

The Farrier said that he would do it and I stipulated one bullet only because I had seen so many trembling hands and their results.

Later that day I visited a working party engaged in salvaging cable and when the rations and water came later, one of the men enquired if I was having my horse shot, because he had seen the Farrier leading him, with Corporal Cook holding his rifle and they were near some old trenches.

So I replied, 'If anyone asks, you never saw that.'

'Oh' he replied, 'all the men know and think it's a good idea. They don't want him left here.' Nevertheless, I asked the man to keep it to himself. I knew that if anyone spoke to me about it I would break down, and didn't want this to happen in front of my men.

When I returned to the encampment the Farrier said they led Timbuc into the trench and placed the rifle against his white star and pulled the trigger. Killing him instantly and filling in the soil round him.

So ended the life of a friendly, intelligent, noble animal, whose speed had, at times, been the means of saving me from capture by the enemy.

That week was one of the saddest of my life. I did not eat all week, and I never went to the horse lines again. I left all those duties to a Sergeant. I was heartbroken but the war had ended and men were being demobilised, thousands of horses were being shot.

I had lost my best friend, Timbuc, a horse of spirit, who was so very lovable. But his memory remains constant and I have cried over my decision many times. If only I could have brought him home. If only.

I never rode a horse again in my life.

Postscript

My grandfather's mother and his sister, Annie, both lived into their 90s. His younger sister, Winnie, drowned in 1942, and not long afterwards his brother, Joseph, died of cancer.

In April 1976, Norman and Clara celebrated their golden wedding anniversary. Two years later, Clara died from breast cancer. My grandfather was truly heartbroken. After this he moved to live near us in Taunton and began to write poetry, and to write his memoirs.

He died peacefully at Netherclay House, near Taunton, on 11th October 1987.

Grandpa, 1987

Bibliography

Books:

1. *The Sleepwalkers: How Europe Went to War in 1914.* Christopher Clark. Penguin Books, 2013
2. *Edwardian England, 1901-15: Society and Politics.* Donald Read. Harrap, 1972
3. *The Berlin-Baghdad Express: The Ottoman Empire and Germany's Bid for World Power.* Sean McMeekin. Harvard University Press, 2010
4. *Hankey: Man of Secrets. Vol 2.* Stephen W. Roskill. Collins, 1972
5. *The Great War 1914-1918.* Peter Hart. Profile Books, 2014
6. *The Technology of World War I.* Stewart Ross. Raintree Steck-Vaughn Publishers, 2003
7. *The Dardanelles Disaster: Winston Churchill's Greatest Failure.* Dan Van der Vat. Penguin, 2010
8. *The Uncensored Dardanelles.*[Illustrated edition]. Ellis Ashmead-Bartlett. Edition published by Pickle Partners Publishing from text originally published by Hutchinson & Co Ltd, 1928
9. *Gallipoli Diary Volume I.* Sir Ian Hamilton. Edward Arnold, 1920 URL: http://www.gutenberg.org/ebooks/19317

10. *Gallipoli Diary Volume 2*. Sir Ian Hamilton. Edward Arnold, 1920 URL: http://www.gutenberg.org/ebooks/22021

11. *The Defence of Gallipoli*. George S. Patton Jr. HQ Hawaiian Dept. 1936. URL: http://books.google.co.uk/books/about/The Defense of Gallipoli.html?id=FdZDnQEACAAJ&redir_esc=y

12. *Gallipoli*. Alan Moorehead. Wordsworth Military Library, 1997

13. *Gallipoli*. Michael Hickey. John Murray Publishers, 1995

14. *Gallipoli*: The Ottoman Campaign. Edward J. Erickson. Pen and Sword Military, 2010

15. *Gallipoli*. Les Carlyon. Macmillan, 2003

16. *Gully Ravine*: Gallipoli. Stephen Chambers. Pen & Sword, 2002

17. *Suvla: the August Offensive*. Stephen J. Chambers. Pen & Sword, 2011

18. *Gallipoli: The Landing at Helles*. Huw & Jill Rodge. Pen & Sword, 2003

19. *The Battle for Palestine 1917*. John D. Grainger. Boydell Press, 2006

20. *When God Made Hell: The British Invasion of Mesopotamia and the Creation of Iraq*, 1914-1921. Charles Townshend. Faber & Faber, 2010

21. *Hundred Days: The End of the Great War*. Nick Lloyd. Penguin Books, 2013

22. *Hero: The Life and Legend of Lawrence of Arabia*. Micael Korda, Sachs R. JR books; 2011

23. *Setting the Desert on Fire: T.E. Lawrence and Britain's Secret War in Arabia*. James Barr. Bloomsbury Publishing; 2007

24. *Eden to Armageddon: World War One in the Middle East.* Roger Ford. Orion Books, 2007

25. Eye-Deep in Hell: Life in the Trenches 1914-1918. John Ellis. Fontana/Collins, 1977.

Papers:

Technological Adaptation in Global Conflict: The British Army and Communications Beyond the Western Front 1914-1918. Brian N. Hall. *The Journal of Military History.* 78 (January 2014): 523-556. http://www.salford.ac.uk/arts-media/arts-media-academics/brian-hall

Conditions: Evacuation of the Sick and Wounded from Gallipoli. Sarah Paterson. Imperial War Museum. September 2000. URL: http://archive.iwm.org.uk/upload/package/2/gallipoli/pdf_files/MedEvac.pdf

Helles: The French in Gallipoli. Eleanor van Heyningen. Imperial War Museum. September 2000. URL: http://archive.iwm.org.uk/upload/package/2/gallipoli/pdf_files/French.pdf

Internet Sources (all live at the time of publication):

The road to war

http://www.historytoday.com/john-etty/serbian-nationalism-and-great-war

http://madmonarchist.blogspot.co.uk/2012/08/soldier-of-monarchy-field-marshal-franz.html

Conditions for the soldiers on Gallipoli

http://www.anzacday.org.au/history/ww1/anecdotes/casualty.html

Developments in military technology

http://www.firstworldwar.com/airwar/observation.htm
http://www.firstworldwar.com/weaponry/gas.htm
http://www.historyplace.com/worldhistory/firstworldwar/index-1915.html

The Thrill and the Horror

http://www.greatwar.co.uk/medals/ww1-gallantry-awards.htm

The Western Libyan Desert and the Senussids

http://query.nytimes.com/gst/abstract.html?res=9A00E1D7153D
EF3ABC4152DFB566838D609EDE
http://query.nytimes.com/mem/archive-free/pdf?res=F50A10F63
E591A7A93CBA81788D85F428185F9
http://books.google.co.uk/books?id=w8lNaPldEZAC&pg=PA7&l
pg=PA7&dq=Moorina+and+Tara&source=bl&ots=LFJfjRx7ts&si
g=LcCzijr2fnjueC69mWWkVxVnwnc&hl=en&sa=X&ei=m7MU
U83rCOme7Abw84Ag&ved=0CEcQ6AEwBA#v=onepage&q=Mo
orina%20and%20Tara&f=false

http://www.1914-1918.net/wff.htm

Life in the Army in the Desert

http://www.awm.gov.au/collection/ART40979/
http://www.theglobalmail.org/feature/war-and-pieces/468/

The Sinai Desert and the Battle for Romani

Current U.S. Military Fluid Replacement Guidelines. Margaret A. Kolka, Ph.D., William A. Latzka, Sc.D.2, Scott J. Montain, Ph.D. and Michael N. Sawka, Ph.D. United States Army Research Institute of Environmental Medicine, Kansas Street Natick, MA 01760-5007, USA and Department of Chemistry and Life Sciences U.S. Military Academy, West Point, NY 10996 USA: http://hprc-online.org/nutrition/hprc-articles/files/current-u-s-military-fluid-replacement

Water Intake and Urine Output During a 194-Kilometre Unsupported Desert March http://ftp.rta.nato.int/public/PubFullText/RTO/MP/RTO-MP-HFM-086/MP-HFM-086-07.pdf VR Nevola, QinetiQ Centre for Human Sciences; MA Stroud OBE, University of Southampton Department of Clinical Nutrition; Maj. JJ Turner, RE Defence Logistics Organisation, Andover; WR Withey QinetiQ Centre for Human Sciences Cody technology Park, Farnborough UK

Commanders' Guide to Portable Fluid Intake During Military Duty in Hot Environments. V René Nevola, Dstl. 26th June 2008: http://www.science.mod.uk/codex/issue1/journals/journals3.aspx

The Western Front 1918

http://archive.org/stream/ordealofwoodroww028046mbp/ordealofwoodroww028046mbp_djvu.txt

The Decauville steam locomotive: http://www.youtube.com/watch?v=VgiXS8l6G20 and http://www.internationalsteam.co.uk/trains/france03.htm

Index